Guiding Light

The Soul Who Could

CYCLE A

Homilies by Fr. Joe Robinson

Shepherds of Christ Publications
P.O. Box 627
Madison (China), Indiana 47250 USA

Toll free USA: (888) 211-3041
Tel: (812) 273-8405
Fax: (812) 273-3182
Email: info@sofc.org
http://www.sofc.org

First Printing: 2016

Dedicated to Pope Francis

In Honor of Our Beloved Priests

98th Anniversary of Fatima
October 13, 2015

My dear priests, hierarchy and members of the mystical body of Christ,

I give my heart to Jesus and Mary with you in love.

Fr. Carter our founder wrote two very important books *Response to God's Love* and *Response in Christ*.

The following thoughts are inspired by these two books.

God first loved us.

We receive a sharing in Divine Life in baptism – our knowing and loving capacity is elevated.

We are human creatures and yet we see God's loving self-communication to us with our concomitant response to Him in love.

Man rejected this self-communication of God in original sin.

God on His part communicates His own life through grace and man in return gives himself to God and his fellowman in loving service.

We can respond to this marvelous gift God gives to us as members of the mystical body of Christ – with Christ our head.

We can be witnesses of Christ alive in us both in the Church and in the world because the Father, Son and Holy Spirit dwell in a special way, in our graced, baptized soul.

God wants such intimacy with us.

I, Rita Robinson Ring, have learned a lot about the spiritual life from Our Lord in daily Mass and in spending at least one hour a day before the Blessed Sacrament where Jesus is truly present in His Divinity and humanity, no less present than when He walked the earth.

I have been guided by Fr. Carter our founder and had the gift of my brother, Fr. Joe Robinson at Mass, Sunday, week days, funerals etc. and other priests who have helped us on our journey in Shepherds of Christ.

Through the Priestly Newsletter of Fr. Carter we circulated 17,000,000 Newsletters to Priests and Hierarchy since 1994. This is Fr. Joe's 9th book. We sent out most years to about 38,000 priests and hierarchy. We have circulated about 300,000 of Fr. Joe's homily books over 8 years to priests and hierarchy.

What a gift these homilies of Fr. Joe's are as he teaches us about Responding to God's love, being Christ a-live in this world as a witness to Jesus and teaching us about the Bread of Life: the Word and the Eucharist.

We pray for the priests and have since 1994 in prayer chapters. Our prayers have been translated in 8 languages with the *Imprimatur*. We especially pray 8 days every month with Mass and the Holy Eucharist exposed most of the days for the priests, the Church and the world. We pray 24 hours every day and night in China before the exposed Eucharist for the priests and the Church.

Please pray with us, the prayers, Fr. Carter, our Founder, gave us in 1994 centered in Consecration to the Hearts of Jesus and Mary praying for the priests, the Church and the world. Life is in Jesus.

With love,
Rita Robinson Ring and all at Shepherds of Christ

We want Adoration Chapels
around the world –
The Mighty Medicine

Table of Contents
Cycle A – 2016 / 2017

Certificate of Marriage

I, the undersigned, do hereby certify, that on the 25 day of June A.D. 19 36
in the church of St. Boniface I joined in the

Holy Bonds of Matrimony

William M. Robinson and Alice Weber

according to the rites of the Holy Roman Catholic Church.

Witness: Henry J. Robinson
Marie Weber

Rev. John H. Schwartz
Pastor

Dedicated to William and Alice Robinson.

Our Mother and Father married on
June 25, 1936 in St. Boniface Church, Cincinnati.

1st Sunday of Advent
December 1, 2013

INTRODUCTION – (Isaiah 2,1-5; Romans 13,11-14; Matthew 24,37-44) The prophet we hear in today's first reading lived over 700 years before Christ. Most probably he had witnessed the destruction of the northern kingdom of Israel by the Assyrians, fierce warriors who came from what is modern day Iraq. The southern kingdom of Israel, centered in Jerusalem, lived in fear and trembling that the same fate awaited them. In spite of great turmoil, his message is a message of peace, a peace we continue to yearn for. It is a peace, however, that we find only when we walk in God's ways.

HOMILY – A little boy was asked in Sunday school what he was going to give his little sister for Christmas. He said "I don't know." The teacher asked, "well, what did you give her last year?" The little boy said "chicken pox." Let's hope this Christmas he comes up with something nicer! The Joyful Noiseletter, Dec. 2011.

I do not get to plays or musicals very often, but a week ago went with a few friends to see Fiddler on the Roof. One of the memorable songs in it is "Sunrise, Sunset." The Jewish father was marrying off his eldest daughter, and he couldn't understand where the time went. In his mind she was still his little girl playing with her friends. I can't repeat all the words of the song, but this line I do remember, and it is appropriate for today, the first Sunday of Advent: "Sunrise, sunset, sunrise, sunset, swiftly flow the years, one season following the other, laden with happiness and tears." Today we begin a new Church year and in a month we begin a new calendar year. Where does the time go? We do not like to think about this, but for all of us the day will come when we will have no more days left.

Our liturgy reminds us of this, because when our time in this world has ended, a new life, eternal life is ahead for us. The gospels recall some of the things Jesus said about this end time. It recalls things Jesus said about the end of Jerusalem, the destruction of the Temple, the end of the world as we know it now and the second coming of Christ. Two weeks ago we heard about the destruction of the Temple. Today the focus is on the coming of the Son of Man; that is, the second coming of Christ. We will be busy in the next few weeks getting ready to celebrate the birth of Jesus, but the Church wants us to also get ready for the coming of the adult Jesus who will establish forever God's kingdom of peace and love.

The gospels insist no one knows when that will happen. People have been predicting Jesus' second coming for 2000 years, and they've all been wrong. St. Paul gives us some idea of what it will be like when it does take place. Paul's description of the second coming was in response to the fear that the Thessalonians had that their loved ones who had died would miss out on the great event when Jesus would come again. I would like to quote what he tells us in I Thessalonians: "Indeed, we tell you this, on the word of the Lord, that we who are alive, who are left until the coming of the Lord, will surely not precede those who have fallen asleep (i.e. relatives and friends who have died). For the Lord himself, with a word of command, with the voice of an archangel and with the trumpet of God, will come down from heaven, and the dead in Christ will rise first. Then we who are alive, who are left, will be caught up together with them in the clouds to meet the Lord in the air. Thus we shall always be with the Lord." (I Thessalonians, 4,15-17) (Translation taken from New American Bible)

Today's gospel does not give us such a clear picture of the second coming, but it does give us a message that is extremely important: don't let his second coming catch you by surprise. Jesus tells us it will be like the flood at the time of Noah: no one was ready for it except Noah and his family; it will be like a robbery, no one gets a notice from the thief saying what day or time he or she will show up. The example of the two men working in the field or the two women grinding at the mill shows the suddenness with which it will happen; it also infers one out of each pair would be marked for salvation and one for judgment because one was ready and one was not.

How can we be ready? I suggest we ask ourselves what would we do if we knew for sure Christ was returning to earth in his second coming this year on December 25. Perhaps we would spend a little more time in prayer, or reading the gospels, or going to confession, or coming to Holy Hour or morning Mass during the week, or doing some charitable works. Maybe if we can't think of anything special to do, we could ask our Lord for a suggestion, then quietly wait for an answer. This time of the year is a busy time and before we know it Christmas will be here and gone and we'll be remembering the theme of "Sunrise, Sunset," and wondering where the day and weeks have disappeared to.

2nd Sunday of Advent
December 8, 2013

INTRODUCTION – (Isaiah 11,1-10; Romans 15,4-9; Matthew 3,1-12) The historical setting for today's first reading goes back 700 years before Christ. It was a time of great distress for Israel. The Assyrians had literally annihilated all of the area north of Jerusalem, an area known as the northern kingdom. It was very likely Jerusalem would be the next victim of the Assyrian army. In spite of all this, we hear in today's reading a message of hope - a promise of great blessings to those who have remained faithful to God. A great leader, filled with the Spirit of God, would usher in these blessings. This leader would come from the royal house of David - that is what Isaiah meant when he identifies this leader as "a shoot that would sprout from the stump of Jesse." Jesse was the father of King David, as I'm sure you all know, and the kingship in Jerusalem was barely surviving as the word "stump" indicates.

HOMILY – I am going to present my homily in two parts: first I'll say some things about John the Baptist; second I want to say something about his message.

First, a little background about John the Baptist. St. Luke tells us his parents were Elizabeth and Zechariah. John was born to them miraculously when they were old, a sign that John would be a special gift from God. Zechariah was a priest who served at the Jerusalem Temple and Elizabeth was a relative of Mary, Jesus' mother. Luke chose to use the word "relative" rather than the word "cousin," which gives one the idea that Elizabeth and Mary were more distant relatives. Now we are going to do a little reading between the lines, speculations that scholars have made about John and Jesus. We suspect there was not very much contact between the two of them or between John and Jesus when they were growing up because in the fourth gospel John said of Jesus, "I myself did not know him, but the one who sent me to baptize with water said to me, 'He on whom you see the Spirit descend and remain is the one who baptizes with the Holy Spirit." (John 1,33) It is a good guess that after John's parents died, John was raised by and was part of the community of the Essenes, the people responsible for writing the Dead Sea Scrolls. It is likely that John got the idea of baptizing people from the Essenes. It is fair to speculate that John separated from the Essenes because of his belief that the Messiah's coming was imminent, that the kingdom of heaven was "fast approaching;" and the need for reform was urgent. (The Gospel of Matthew, Anchor Bible, pg 28) Many scholars have speculated that Jesus participated in John's ministry for a short time before he went off on his own. Now I go back to information we get directly from the gospels. John's ascetical lifestyle is well known. He lived in the desert, dressed like the great prophet Elijah and ate wild honey and locusts (locust refers to the bug, which is high in vitamins and is still eaten today by people in the Middle East. I think I would rather eat broccoli!) The most important thing to remember about John is that he was a great prophet. Jesus said of him: "Amen, I say to you, among those born of women no one has arisen greater than John the Baptist." (Mt. 11,11) To conclude what I have to say about John, like most prophets, John was put to death because he offended those in power at the time.

As a prophet, God spoke through John and so the Church chooses today's reading because through them, God is now speaking to us. I think if there is any time in history John's message needs to be heard it is that it needs to be heard by people in today's culture. John's message was to repent, which means to have a change of heart. This means we need to have God first in our lives, not second or third or fourth, but first. When John said "do not say 'We have Abraham for our father,'" John was telling the Jews you can't presume because you are a member of God's chosen people you can do whatever you want without the possibility of any negative consequences. John is telling us, too, that we can't do what we want or make up our own rules just because we carry the name Catholic. It drives me crazy when I see people on the news who engage in outlandish behavior and then say they are Catholic. So what. Does that make their behavior okay? Or the same is true of those who claim "I don't have any religion but I'm a spiritual person," as many do today. Which is their way of saying I can live the way I want, and because I'm "spiritual" it's okay. It's God who makes the rules, not us. John says we, like a tree, must bear good fruit which means we must live a virtuous life and let God's law and God's Spirit guide our lives. It is an important message for Advent. As Christmas draws near, we can have parties and give gifts and send cards and decorate and bake, but as Thomas Merton writes "it's important to remember the deep seriousness of Advent, which should remind us that the King who is to come is more than a charming infant smiling in the straw. The Advent mystery focuses the light of faith upon the very meaning of life, of history, of humanity, of the world and of our own being." (Seasons of Celebration)

John's call to put God first is the same message that came from Jesus. One of the ways we do this is to put him first by giving him an hour of our time at the beginning of the week. Where will our lives of virtue lead us? The answer is right there in the first reading - to a new world, a world led by God's own Spirit, a world where justice will rule and where there will be peace. As we wait for that day to come, we must prepare for it now, John said, by living holy lives. Amen.

Feast of the Immaculate Conception
December 8, 2005

HOMILY – (Gen. 3:9-15, 20; Luke 1:26-38) The feast today is about Mary's conception, that from the instant she began to exist on this earth, indeed from her very conception, she was holy, filled with God's grace and without sin. The gospel today can confuse us somewhat because it tells us about Jesus' conception. It was read today, first of all, because there is no gospel telling us about the moment when Mary was conceived. And secondly today's gospel does give us an important piece of information about Mary related to today's feast. The angel greeted her as: "Full of grace." Our feast celebrates what the angel stated. There was no moment in Mary's life when God's grace did not fill her. She was full of grace.

As we listen in on this conversation between Mary and the Angel, we learn not only about Mary but also about the child she is going to have. Mary's son to be would be Son of the Most High and king forever. Her child will be called "holy, the Son of God." In the midst of all our business, we pause on this Holy Day to think what it is we are happy about at this time of year.

This is why Mary was "full of grace," so she could give birth to the source of all holiness and grace, God's own Son. And why did he come to us? So that we too can become holy. This is what St. Paul tells us in today's second reading: "God chose us in him to be holy and blameless in his sight."

Holiness is something few people strive for. All of us want to get to heaven, but most of us would probably tend to say I just want to get inside the door. We should do more than just try to get inside the door. We are called to be holy. Most of us never think that becoming holy is our vocation. We usually think holiness is for someone else, like the saints or people in religious orders. That's because we do not understand holiness. We think being holy means spending all day praying or wearing ourselves out doing good things for others and never having a chance to have any fun. I think holy people probably have as much fun as any of us, but there's something greater than fun. It is joy and peace and love. To be holy means to be close to God. The closer we are to God, the more we will be filled with love and joy and peace – both in this life and throughout eternity.

Our vocation to holiness is illustrated by the two stories we heard today.

The first story was about our first parents who originally were very close to God and were very happy. That was the symbolism of the Garden of Eden. But that wasn't good enough for them. They wanted to be like God himself. So they rebelled against God and they lost all they had.

The second story, the Annunciation, illustrates Mary's constant attitude of being willing to say "yes" to God. It was only through her openness that the Son of the Most High has come to us. St. Luke tells us Mary was not only holy and always ready to do whatever God wanted of her, but he also tells us she was joyful. Holiness and joy are connected. After the angel left Mary, St. Luke told us about Mary visiting her cousin and she was full of joy. She expressed her joy in the beautiful hymn "the Magnificat." "My soul gives glory to the Lord and my spirit rejoices in God my savior."

In reflecting on the holiness of Mary, we may feel as if we were treated unfairly. We were born with original sin. The deck was stacked against us from the beginning. But we forget that when we were baptized we were filled with

God's life. The very same grace that filled Mary at the moment of her conception, filled us when we were baptized. So holiness is possible for us too. Our two stories can show us there are two ways each of us can go in life. We can follow the example of our first parents, Adam and Eve, or we can follow the example of Mary. The first will lead to sorrow, the other to joy. To imitate Mary, all we have to do is say "yes" to whatever God asks of us.

3rd Sunday of Advent
December 15, 2013

INTRODUCTION – (Isaiah 35,1-6a.10; James 5,7-10; Matthew 11,2-11) If you or I could change our world to make it better, what would we do to change it? Today Isaiah describes to God's people (most probably those who were still in exile) what God's plans were to make things better for them. God would start with the land, turning their desert, arid lands into gardens bursting with vegetation and beauty, comparable to the costal areas where the land was fertile and there was adequate rainfall, such as Lebanon, Carmel (which is today Haifa) and Sharon. Transforming the land was just a beginning. Those who were weak, sick, blind and lame would be freed of their affliction. It would be a return to the Garden of Eden where God's people would be crowned with everlasting joy. What a beautiful picture of salvation Isaiah presents. Matthew tells us in today's gospel that God's work of creating a new world begins with Jesus. St. James tells us in the second reading that as we hope for a new world, we must be patient and steadfast in our faith.

HOMILY – Christmas is near, the liturgy tells us to rejoice! Christmas is that time of the year when a person sits in front of a dead tree and eats candy out of his/her sock." Victor Borge had this to say about Christmas: "Santa Claus has the right idea. Visit people only once a year." (The Joyful Noiseletter, Nov./Dec. 2013, pg 2) Well, we had to have a little humor today - after all, today is Gaudete Sunday. "Gaudete" means rejoice. It is true, the celebration of his birth is just a week and a half away, but the Lord himself is near as we gather together in faith to hear his word and to receive him in the Sacrament. That is always a cause for rejoicing. As we say in the Mass every day, "Lift up your hearts."

It is our faith and hope in God's promises, promises yet to be fully realized, and it is our confidence in his love that are the source of our joy. In the first reading we hear the prophet, this prophet known as deutero-Isaiah or second Isaiah, a prophet who lived during the time of the Babylonian exile. The prophet promises God would restore his people to their homes and their world itself would be transformed. We know that we, too, are away from our true home now (which is heaven as St. Paul tells us - Philippians 2,20), but when we arrive there our world will be transformed also, transformed so wonderfully that we have no way to fully describe it. We do know we will be really fulfilled and happy - forever!

As James tells us, until that day when God brings us to our heavenly dwelling, we have to wait in patience and faith. That's what John the Baptist was doing as he sat in prison - trying to be patient, and perhaps trying to hold on to his faith. No one knows how to interpret John's psychological state when he sent his disciples to ask Jesus: "Are you the one who is to come?" Was he beginning to develop faith in Jesus or was he beginning to lose what faith he had or was he interested only in introducing his disciples to Jesus? No one can say what he was feeling. My own suspicion is since Jesus proclaimed that he had come to "give release to the captives," (Lk. 4,18) John was confused about Jesus. Jesus was doing all these wonderful things that Isaiah talks about: healing the blind, the deaf, the lame, the mute, but here was John, still locked up in prison. Why, if Jesus was the "one who is to come," didn't he rescue John? I think that's what was behind John's question.

The question John asks is one I am sure every one of us has asked at different times throughout our lives. Are you the "one who is to come," the promised one who will save us. On this we come back to our second reading: "Be patient, the coming of the Lord is very close." If I ever find out why bad things happen to good people, I'll write a book, but until then I'll keep believing in Jesus - there's no other answer to life's ups and downs as far as I'm concerned, and that is where I find my joy. Amen.

4th Sunday of Advent
December 22, 2013

INTRODUCTION – (Isaiah 7:10-14; Romans 1:1-7; Matthew 1:18-24) Our first reading takes us back 700 years before Christ to the Middle East. It was as complicated a political situation then as it is today. There are four nations and their kings involved in this complicated story I'm going to tell you. Tiglath-pileser III was king over the Assyrians. The Assyrians were the dominant power in the Middle East. They were an especially cruel and powerful nation whose capital was located in what is today northern Iraq. Ahaz was king in Jerusalem, and that's the only name you will need to remember. There were two more kings whose lands were north of Jerusalem. These two kings from the north decided they wanted to go to war against Assyria and they wanted King Ahaz in Jerusalem to join them. Ahaz refused, so the two northern kings were going to attack Jerusalem to replace Ahaz with someone who would go along with their scheme. Ahaz decided to call on Assyria for protection. This is where our first reading comes in - an extremely important passage in the Book of the Prophet Isaiah. Isaiah warned Ahaz not to get involved with Assyria for they were too powerful. Isaiah promised, "God would keep the king and Jerusalem safe." The two kings from the north would soon be destroyed. Ahaz did not have enough faith in God. Isaiah tried to offer Ahaz a sign that he should trust God. Ahaz, in a phony display of humility, protested, but Isaiah offered a sign anyway. For Ahaz the sign would be that he would soon have a son to succeed him as king. He had no offspring at this time for he had recently sacrificed his only son to the Canaanite God, Moloch. This future son of King Ahaz would be called by the symbolic name Emmanuel for he would be a sign that God was with his people. God was faithful to his word. Ahaz did have a son who succeeded him and his son turned out to be a good leader. Almost eight centuries later, St. Matthew saw in this promise of Isaiah a greater depth of meaning as we will hear in today's gospel. He saw that Jesus fulfilled this promise perfectly by being born of a virgin and by being a sign to us that God is with us.

HOMILY – Bob forgot to give his wife a gift or bring her flowers on their wedding anniversary. His wife was really angry. He asked how he could make things right with her. She said with Christmas around the corner, she wanted a gift that would go from 0 to 200 in six seconds. So on Christmas he told her the gift was in the garage. She ran down excitedly, opened the garage door and there in the garage was a brand new, brightly shining, chrome plated bathroom scale. Bob hasn't been seen or heard from since.

It seems to be a guy thing to forget anniversaries. But anniversaries are very important. We are preparing to celebrate the anniversary of the birth of Jesus, an anniversary that people have celebrated for about 17 centuries. Both Matthew and Luke describe for us some of the events leading up to the birth of Jesus. Since most of our gospels this year will be from Matthew's gospel, we listen to what Matthew tells us about Jesus' birth. Matthew's account of Jesus' birth and the events that led up to it does not lend itself to beautiful works of art or musical compositions as does Luke's infancy narrative. We can appreciate Matthew because he tells us what was happening with Joseph, while Luke tells us mostly about Mary. We wish they could have told us more, but these were the traditions they had to work with, so we are grateful for preserving them for us.

Both Matthew and Luke stress the miraculous nature of Jesus' conception and the problems it created for Mary and Joseph. To understand what was happening with Joseph, we have to know that for the Jews, marriage took place in two stages. First there was a formal exchange of consent before witnesses. The second step was at a later time (usually about a year later) when the groom took the bride to his home. Even before they came to live together, legally they were considered married. Problems arose when Mary conceived Jesus before they lived together. Joseph didn't know what to do, at least not until the angel told him, "Joseph, son of David, do not be afraid to take Mary your wife into your home." Of course, he obeyed the message of the angel. Until the angel spoke to him, we do not know what Joseph was thinking. I can't imagine that Mary didn't tell him what was happening, but whether Joseph didn't believe what she told him and he thought she had been unfaithful, or whether he did believe her and he felt unworthy to be part of such a holy event, we are not told. Matthew doesn't give us any insight into Joseph's decision to divorce Mary. Matthew's main intent is to tell us of the miraculous nature of Jesus' birth and that Joseph had a necessary part to play as he was "son of David" (the title the angel gave him in his dream). Legally he would be Jesus' father, he would give Jesus his name (which he did) and legally Jesus would belong to the royal house of David. As a member of the royal house of David, Jesus would fulfill the Messianic expectations of God's people and he would fulfill the ancient prophecy of Nathan, the prophet who told David (1000 years earlier) that "God would establish the throne of David's kingdom forever." (II Samuel, 7,13)

Our gospel is interesting in that it confirms the miraculous conception of Jesus and it gives us a little more insight about the events that surrounded Jesus' birth, but in addition our gospel has a message for us today. It shows us how our lives can take a sudden turn. We have our life planned out and we're going along peacefully day by day doing what we had intended and then, without warning, everything is turned upside down: perhaps it is a sudden sickness or death, a financial loss, a new child within the family, a new in-law or whatever. (thoughts from Biblical Meditations for Advent and the Christmas Season by Carroll Stuhlmueller, pg 70) We are reminded we are not in charge and we have to fall back on our faith that God loves us and will help us get through whatever situation we are in. Only God saves (which is what the name "Jesus" means: Yahweh saves). Amen.

Christmas
December 25, 2013

HOMILY – Tom was fresh out of ideas as to what to get his mother-in-law for Christmas. So he bought her a large plot in an expensive cemetery. The following Christmas he also couldn't think of anything to get her, so he didn't buy her anything. She complained he was so thoughtless and was just taking her for granted. He said "what are you complaining about? You still haven't used the present I gave you last year." (My apologies to all mother-in-laws for that one, 99% of whom are all wonderful, loving persons).

A first grader told her classmates that Santa lived in China. When her teacher heard that, she asked the little girl why she thinks Santa lives in China. She said all her gifts say "made in China."

When two little boys came to visit their grandmother and spend an overnight at her home, as they were saying their prayers, one of the two boys started loudly shouting his prayers: "God, please send me a video game and a new bike." His brother asked why he was shouting, "God isn't deaf." The first little boy said "but grandma almost is."

This is a time of the year when there is new hope, new joy, a new attitude of care and concern for one another. It is a time of the year when many people are overwhelmed with stress and guilt, stress in trying to do too much and guilt in not being able to do it. It is a time of year when, if a person has suffered some sadness or loss in the past, even in spite of the hope this season offers, the sense of sadness seems much more acute. It is, in brief, a very emotional time and hopefully 99% of you are feeling God's joy and peace.

Every Christmas we hear the same story, how the Son of God took on our human flesh and lived among us, how he revealed the kingdom of God to us, a kingdom of peace and love, a kingdom free from suffering, a kingdom of eternal joy. It is a kingdom that is beyond anything we can imagine or anything in this world that we can compare it with. His coming to live among us has changed the world forever. Even though there are those who do not believe in him or even hate him, they cannot change the fact that our world is different because Jesus was born and over 2 billion people (over 1/4 of the world's population) believe in him and follow him.

Every Christmas we hear the same story, but every year we hear it somewhat differently because in the course of a year we have become different. For better or for worse, we are not exactly the same person we were last year this time. We may have grown stronger or weaker, we may have learned more or forgotten more, we may have made new friends or lost old friends, our health may have improved or declined. I was thinking how my attitudes about Christmas have changed over the years - from a very materialistic kid who wanted to make sure he didn't get slighted when Christmas gifts were passed around to become, I hope, a more spiritually oriented person who stands in awe before the crib, wondering that God did this for us, grateful for his goodness and looking at the face of the infant and knowing I am looking right into the face of God.

One of the psalm refrains for Christmas says: "today is born our savior, Christ the Lord." That word "today" keeps running through my mind. Sure Christ was born a little over 2000 years ago, but today he is born for each one of us. As we go through life, he keeps coming to us, he keeps inviting us to get to know him better, he keeps offering us a sharing in his own divine life, eternal life.

Today he comes to each of us to the degree that we can open our hearts to him. Today he comes to us in those we love, in those we forgive, in those who cause us distress, in those we serve and care for. Today he comes to us in prayer, especially in the greatest prayer we have, the Mass, where we listen to his Word and where he offers us himself as our spiritual food and drink.

His birth has changed the world. May he change all of us for the better, making us aware of his presence, his love, his eternal grace and helping us to be faithful to him. Amen.

Feast of the Holy Family
December 30, 2007

HOMILY – (Sirach 3:3-7, 14-17a, Colossians 3:12-21, Matthew 2:13-15, 19-23) Just a few days ago we heard St. Luke describe the birth of Jesus at Bethlehem. Although the manger may not have been the Ritz, we imagined a scene described in the song: Silent night, Holy night. The silence of that night was broken only by the angels praising God and announcing peace to God's people on earth. Now we hear Matthew's gospel.

The peace and quiet are gone. The paranoid king, Herod the Great, is intent on destroying the child Jesus and the Holy Family have to escape by leaving their own homeland and becoming refugees in neighboring Egypt. It's like a splash of cold water in the face, but this splash is really a splash of cold reality, reminding us that no family, not even the holiest has a stress-free existence. It also reminds us of the universal conflict and tension between the forces of good and evil, light and darkness, grace and sin. The forces of evil lined up against Jesus right from the beginning. Matthew's story also reminds us that although our decision to follow Jesus takes us along a road that leads to eternal happiness, that road is not always paved or smooth.

Our focus today is on the family. The importance of the family cannot be overstated or over emphasized. The family is where we discover what it means to be human, what are our strengths and weaknesses, where we experience love and forgiveness, where we learn about relationships, unity, sacrifice, loving others, accepting others, where we learn values and attitudes and trust and how to handle stress and how to be responsible. Family is where we learn how to get along with one another. All these important learning tasks are hopefully learned in a family that is relatively healthy. I say "relatively healthy" because none of us and none of our families are perfect. A family that is seriously dysfunctional teaches a lot of other things that end up not being very helpful. The success of society depends on the health of the family. That creates a big burden for families to carry. It also puts a big burden on society to care about the family and to foster healthy families. Today we celebrate the importance of another family, our parish family. Here too we discover who we are as God's children, how to trust God and to love God and one another. We learn values here too, values that are intended to lead us into eternal life. Hopefully we learn how to give as well as take, how to forgive as well as be forgiven. Here we gather around a family table to be fed, not with perishable food but with food that will nourish us eternally. Our faith community is just as important in its own way as our family of origin. And the Lord's supper that we share is just as important to our spiritual well being as being together and eating together as a family is to our emotional well being.

Today we celebrate 10 years as the united family of St. Boniface and St. Patrick. Back in 1853 St. Aloysius was founded as the Catholic parish in North Side. It didn't last as such. The area grew and there was not always peace between the Irish and the Germans, so in less than 10 years St. Aloysius became two parishes: St. Boniface and St. Patrick. On December 29, 1991 we formally became once again, a single parish. Since St. Boniface was structurally the stronger of the two and since St. Boniface had a school, St. Patrick parishioners moved here and the move was a good one from practically every aspect. Only a hand full of people that I know of were unhappy about the merger. (We passed out a booklet a few years ago which contains much more history about our parish. Most people probably already have one, but if you do not we have some more at the doors of church.)

It has been my privilege to be pastor here for the ten years since our merger. None of us knows what the future holds, but if I could make a guess, I think for many reasons St. Boniface will be here for a long time. As for myself, if my health holds up and if the Archbishop lets me I would like to be here for at least another six years. By then I will be 70. I do not know what I will do when I turn 70. I will have to reevaluate things when I get there.

I do want to say how grateful I am to have so many people's support. There's only one thing I wish, and that is that more people took seriously the serious obligation to attend Mass weekly. I think that for the most part families are strengthened by meals together. And the Lord's supper is our family meal each week. I have seen too many people, once they get away from going to Mass every week, slowly drift away from their faith. St. Paul gives us a wonderful list of virtues that would enhance and enrich any of our relationships with one another, especially the relationships within our families: compassion, kindness, gentleness, humility, patience, forgiveness, etc. Notice in this short passage he tells us twice to be grateful. The words St. Paul wrote of course were Greek, but you might find it instructive to hear what words he used: the verb he used was "Eucharisteo." And he tells us we are to become "Eucharistos." It is obvious from these words that the Eucharist allows us to perfectly fulfill his mandate. It is a perfect act of thanksgiving because, in a special way, we, as God's sons and daughters, offer thanks in union with God' own Son, Jesus Christ. May we, on this anniversary, give thanks for our family in Christ, and for our own immediate families. May we be strong and healthy families, full of thankfulness, and may we rejoice one day in the home of the one Father we all have in common, our Father in heaven. Amen.

Mary, Mother of God
January 1, 2008

HOMILY – (Numbers 6:22-27; Galatians 4:4-7; Luke 2:16-21) We have an insatiable appetite for new things. We constantly ask one another "What's new?" The media makes big money keeping us up to date on the latest happenings, good or bad. We read catalogues or search the internet to find out what new things are out there. Some new things are worth celebrating: a new cure for cancer, a new car, a new outfit. Some new things we approach with guarded optimism: a new acquaintance, a new teacher, a new president; and some things are cause for no celebration at all: a new pain somewhere, a new bill we were not expecting. Most everyone approaches the new year as a something worth celebrating. Perhaps it's as good an excuse for a party as anything else. Perhaps we know our new year's resolutions are going to make us into that kind of person we've always wanted to be. Or perhaps we're just glad we made it this far. There are any number of reasons people celebrate. At the same time, however, if we are realistic, we know each new year could bring new challenges, new dangers, new sadness, new tragedy. These are not things we want to think about and certainly not things to celebrate. They are things to pray about, and that's one good reason to begin the year right here, right where we are now: asking God's blessings for whatever is ahead.

Our first reading today is one that we are all familiar with as it is often used as our final blessing at Mass. It is a blessing by which Aaron the high priest, the brother of Moses, blessed God's people as they prepared for their journey to the Promised Land. They had been in the desert of Sinai now for a year. God had made a covenant with them and now they have detailed instructions on how to proceed on to the land of Israel, the Promised Land. Their expectations were high as they started out. Unfortunately the journey did not go well. They had the assurance of a close relationship with God, but they easily became dissatisfied with the hardships of their journey. They gave in to fear of what was ahead and complained they would rather be back in Egypt as slaves. The journey they were on required constant trust in God and they found that hard to do. Sometimes God is all we have to rely on.

The difficult moments of our lives call for trust as well. God is taking us on a journey into a new year, into a new chapter in our lives. If we proceed with trust, the journey will go more smoothly. We do have God's blessings on us.

God's blessing is not something we can see. The shepherds saw angels and the baby Jesus. The people of Israel saw miracles after Jesus had grown up. The Apostles saw Jesus after he had risen. We have only a word to depend on, the word of Jesus: "I will be with you always." And we have the special sign of his presence in the Eucharist guaranteed by his word: "This is my body." "This is my blood."

When the shepherds saw Jesus he probably looked pretty much like most any other little baby. They had only the word of the angels to believe he was special. Our host at Mass doesn't look like anything exceptional either, but Jesus' word tells us it is. It is our Lord and our God who nourishes us as we make our journey through life. This is our guarantee that we have God's blessing on us as we travel on. Having this assurance we who believe can celebrate as we begin a new year. May it be truly blessed for all of us. Amen.

Feast of the Epiphany
January 5, 2014

INTRODUCTION – (Isaiah 60:1-6; Ephesians 3:2-3a, 5-6; Matthew 2:1-12) Jerusalem was destroyed by the Babylonians 587 years before Christ and the Jews who were not killed by the Babylonians were taken to Babylon as exiles. Fifty years later, the Persians (people living in modern day Iran) conquered the Babylonians, and they allowed the Jews to return home. What the Jews returned to was still in shambles just as when it had been destroyed 50 years earlier. Rebuilding was extremely difficult. Today's prophet, writing about 500 years before Christ, tries to encourage the people and assure them Jerusalem would again be a great city. He sees Jerusalem becoming the center of spirituality and light for all the world. People would come from everywhere to visit Jerusalem and to be nourished by the spiritual light and life radiating from it. St. Matthew sees this vision fulfilled in the birth of Jesus and the coming of the magi. When you hear the last few lines of today's first reading you will understand why it was chosen for today's feast of the Epiphany.

HOMILY – Two weeks ago we heard St. Matthew's version of Jesus' birth - how St. Joseph was greatly troubled when it was discovered that Mary was going to have a child and he knew it wasn't his. An angel revealed to Joseph that the child was conceived in her through the Holy Spirit and he should not divorce Mary as he was planning on doing. And so Mary gave birth to her child in Bethlehem. In Matthew there is no mention of shepherds or choirs of angels. Matthew does tell us Jesus got some unusual visitors. The Greek word for these visitors is "magoi" which in its English form is "magi." Magi were sometimes magicians but apparently these magi were astrologers. Astrology was held in high regard in that culture. They were people who were viewed as being able to predict the future by studying the stars. Astrology originated in Babylon and most probably the magi were Babylonians or Persians. It was no easy trip they made as Babylon was about 1000 miles from Jerusalem and Persia was even further. It was pretty much taken for granted at that time that the birth of an important person would be marked by some kind of celestial event. The Jews were not the only people who looked forward to the rule of a great king who would bring peace to the world. The whole Mediterranean world at that time looked for such a leader, so one could say with certitude that the birth of a messiah would definitely be marked by some celestial sign.

The idea that the magi themselves were kings, that they were three in number, and that they traveled by camels (which they probably did in order to carry their luggage) were all ideas that arose later on in Christian literature. They are ideas not supported by today's gospel. It is interesting in that the gospel does not even tell us they were Gentiles, which they most likely were. As Gentiles they represent God revealing his Son to all the nations, while the Jewish people, ironically God's chosen people, received the news of the birth of a Messiah with indifference or even hostility. The Jewish indifference to the birth of Jesus is seen in that the Jewish leaders could tell the magi where the messiah was to be born without going to look for him themselves. The hostility that was shown was on the part of Herod who felt threatened by the birth of a king. I guess Herod thought he would live forever. The irony of it is that Herod did not know that the baby that was born came to bring eternal life to all who would accept him and who would believe in him.

Matthew's story makes us ask ourselves how much effort are we willing to put into our journey to find Christ. I fear many Christians are like the Jews in Jerusalem, able to quote the Scriptures and having all the answers about our faith, maybe even having received all the sacraments, and feeling confident we have a ticket straight into heaven. But have we stopped in our journey to find Christ? Have we stopped seeking to offer him homage? Did you notice how often this phrase was used in today's gospel - after traveling 1000 miles through difficult terrain, the magi were intent of finding the Christ child so they could offer him homage and gifts.

Homage, according to the dictionary, means respect or honor given or shown, especially by action. Many believe that our custom of giving gifts at Christmas originated from the magi bringing gifts to Christ. But what can we give Christ? If we read the gospels, he will tell us what he wants, he wants our time on Sunday, he wants our love, and he wants us to love one another.

Finding Christ is an ongoing effort. We may think we've found him, and sometimes we really feel as if we have, then we realize we still have a long way to go. After 30 years of being a priest, I remember I was feeling pretty smug with myself and with my faith. At that time I took a trip to the Holy Land. While I was at the tomb of Lazarus, I discovered I was taking my relationship with Christ pretty much for granted. Standing in that empty tomb gave me an awesome awareness of who Jesus really is. I forgot he is more than just a friend I can run to when I need a favor. He is the origin of all life, he is the God who made the universe, he is the Lord who by a single word can make the dead come alive. He is worthy of all glory and honor (i.e., homage). The experience was so strong, I couldn't even talk about it for a number of years. Like John the Baptist once said about Jesus: "I did not know him." This revelation helped me move just a little further along in my journey to find Christ. And I realize I must still keep going forward. We will never be finished finding him until we find him in eternity. May this new year bring you a little further along the way to find our Lord and may his star continue to guide you. Amen.

Baptism of the Lord
January 12, 2014

INTRODUCTION – (Isaiah 42,1-4.6-7; Acts 10,34-38; Matthew 3,13-17) In today's first reading, the prophet is speaking to God's people in exile in Babylon,

500 years before Christ. In today's passage God introduces his servant to his people; however the servant is not named. God's servant will be a light to the nations, establish justice in the world and liberate captives, all done in a non-violent manner. God has put his spirit on his servant and it's obvious God is quite pleased with his servant. Scholars debate who the Jews might have thought God was speaking of when they heard this passage; but no one, until after Jesus death and resurrection, ever suspected this passage referred to the Messiah. At Jesus' baptism at the beginning of his public ministry, God introduces Jesus to the world as more than his servant, as his beloved son with whom he is well pleased.

HOMILY – I suspect practically everyone has their Christmas decorations packed away by now, and many of you are no doubt wondering why our church still looks the way it does, with flowers, wreaths and the Christmas crib. There is a very simple explanation. While our society begins to celebrate Christmas weeks in advance, the Church liturgy doesn't begin to celebrate Christmas until Christmas Eve, and it ends the celebration of Jesus' birth with the feast of the Baptism of our Lord. Actually the Baptism of our Lord is part of the feast of the Epiphany. The word Epiphany means God is revealing or showing to all people his Son who was born for us. There are many events in the life of Jesus that reveal or show the Son of God to us, but the initial events that reveal Jesus to us are these three. First, the coming of the magi who were led to Jesus by a star. The second is Jesus' baptism when the Holy Spirit came down upon Jesus and God's voice was heard proclaiming Jesus as God's beloved Son. The third event is when Jesus changed water into wine at the wedding feast at Cana, which John tells us is the first of Jesus' miracles. Today the focus is on the second of these events, Jesus' Baptism.

We think it was strange that Jesus was baptized because John the Baptist's baptism was one of repentance. The purpose of Christian baptism also has as one of its purposes to take away sin. Jesus had no sins to repent of, and so it's difficult to understand why he asked John to baptize him. Even John the Baptist thought it was strange that Jesus would want to be baptized. John didn't want to do it. He told Jesus that Jesus should be baptizing him. But Jesus insisted. Jesus said "it is fitting for us to fulfill all righteousness." Jesus' statement meant that Jesus accepting the baptism of John was in accord with God's will, and Jesus was ready to do perfectly whatever God would ask of him. I could spend the next 45 minutes speculating about why Jesus felt that God the Father wanted him to come to John for baptism. But after all the speculation, we still wouldn't have an answer.

The baptism of Jesus, as recorded in the gospel, was primarily to show that Jesus is God's beloved Son, that he was ever faithful to the will of his Father, that he was anointed by the Holy Spirit as Messiah and he was guided by the Spirit in the course of his ministry. "A new age under the power of God has begun." (The Collegeville Bible Commentary, pg 867)

Although Jesus was without sin and was God's Son from all eternity, Jesus' baptism does teach us some things about our own baptism. When we are baptized, we are fundamentally changed; God sends his Spirit into our hearts and we become, at that moment, God's sons and daughters. The Church reminds us of our baptism. For instance, at the Easter vigil by the Easter candle that is always lit during Easter and by the use of holy water. These reminders of baptism help make us aware of who we have become through God's grace, that we are God's sons and daughters and that we are to live always faithful to God's will. Remind yourself of that the next time you bless yourself with holy water and thank God for the gift of his grace that came to us through the Holy Spirit. Amen.

2nd Sunday in Ordinary Time
January 19, 2014

INTRODUCTION – (Isaiah 49,3.5-6; I Cor. 1,1-3; Jn. 1,29-34) Last week, in our first reading, we heard about God's servant who would bring justice and light to the world. We hear again about God's servant, who would lead the people of Israel back to God and bring God's salvation to the ends of the earth. These four passages about God's servant were written over 500 years before Christ. Scholars do not know who the prophet had in mind when the passages were written, but with the advantage of hindsight we see these passages beautifully describe God's perfect servant, Jesus Christ.

HOMILY – I want to talk about sheep today, but before I do I would like to mention something I found very interesting. The Jews at the time of Jesus disdained shepherds but loved sheep. Shepherds were at the bottom of the social ladder. They had a dirty job and they were viewed as a bunch of crooks, stealing from one another or from the owners of the sheep. Ironically, they loved sheep.

Sheep were a big part of the economy. They provided wool for clothing and food for the table, especially on festive occasions. They were offered to God in sacrifice. They are important in today's liturgy because John the Baptist refers to Jesus as the Lamb of God in today's gospel. It's an image that probably doesn't mean much to most people today. Because it is an image the Church uses in its prayers right before Communion, I want to help you understand the symbolism a little better. There are three important references to sheep in the Scriptures that I would like to focus on.

The first reference is the Paschal Lamb. When God was about to set the Hebrews free from their slavery in Egypt about 1300 years before Christ, Moses instructed the people to protect themselves from the last plague, the Angel of Death, that would descend upon the land of Egypt killing every firstborn male in the land. The Hebrews, however, were to take the blood of the lamb and sprinkle it on the doorpost of their houses and the Angel of Death would pass over those homes. Thus the Hebrews were saved by the blood of a lamb. They were then to roast the lamb and eat it as a family, a meal that became an annual commemoration of God setting his people free. This became "the great national feast of Israel which celebrated its establishment as the people of God." (Dictionary of the Bible, John L. McKenzie, S.J. pg 644)

The second reference is to the Suffering Servant of Isaiah. The four sections of Isaiah that describe the Suffering Servant are known as the Servant Songs because of their poetic style. We heard today that the servant had an awesome responsibility, to "bring [God's] salvation to the ends of the earth." (Is. 49,6) This would be accomplished through the servant's suffering and rejection. The prophet quotes God's people as saying: "While we thought of him as stricken, as one smitten by God and afflicted (for his own sins, yet), he was pierced for our offenses, crushed for our sins. By his stripes we were healed. (Is. 53,4-5) Those who attend services on

Good Friday might recognize those lines. The prophet goes on to say (and this is the important line for our purposes): "Like a lamb led to the slaughter or a sheep before the shearers, he was silent and opened not his mouth. Through his suffering, my servant will justify many, and their guilt he shall bear." (Is 53,7.11) Five hundred years before Christ, these lines were written. They were never thought of as applying to the Messiah for the people imagined the Messiah to be a king or a priest who would be a glorious leader and a powerful, victorious figure - not a suffering one. It was only after Jesus death and resurrection that these servant songs were seen to apply to Jesus the Messiah. But the Baptist, the greatest among the prophets, may have been given this insight that Jesus was the Servant of the Lord when he referred to Jesus as the Lamb of God. Some scholars would argue about this and say that the Baptist referred to Jesus as the "Servant of God" rather than the "Lamb of God" based on the fact that the Aramaic word for lamb is also the word for servant (talya). They suggest that Lamb of God is really a mistranslation - an idea that takes us into a whole different direction.

Our third reference from the Book of Revelation clearly combines the suffering servant with the symbol of the lamb when Jesus is described in this quote from Rev. 5,6: "Then I saw standing in the midst of the throne and the four living creatures and the elders a Lamb that seemed to have been slain. He had seven horns and seven eyes." The seven horns and seven eyes indicate he had the fullness of power and knowledge. Lamb is the main title for Christ in Revelations. All that I have talked about comes together here with the image of the lamb who was slain who is now reigning on high. He is the lamb who died for our sins and whose blood saved us from eternal death. Toward the end of the Book of

Revelation, the author tells us the wedding day of the Lamb has come (i.e., a symbol of God's reign when God will wipe every tear from our eyes, and there shall be no more death or mourning, wailing or pain). Then the angel said to the author of the Book: "write this: Blessed are those who have been called to the wedding feast of the Lamb." (Rev. 19,9) We say something similar right before Communion, that we are called to the supper of the Lamb. I regret that the liturgy uses the word "supper" instead of "wedding feast." "Supper" sounds so mundane. A wedding feast is a grand event. If Jesus worked his first miracle at a wedding feast of changing water into wine just to keep the party going, you might imagine that when God would throw a wedding feast for his Son, the feasting would go on forever. The Eucharist we celebrate is food for our journey and prepares us for this event. Amen.

3rd Sunday in Ordinary Time
January 26, 2014

INTRODUCTION – (Isaiah 8,23-9,3; I Corinthians 1,10-13.17; Matthew 4,12-23) Galilee is located about 75 miles north of Jerusalem. With cars and expressways, that's not very far at all. Since most people traveled on foot at the time of Jesus, it took a few days to make a 75-mile trip. Consequently, Galilee was often forgotten or looked down upon by the religious leaders in Jerusalem. Seven hundred years before Christ, the Assyrians conquered Galilee. Those Jews they didn't kill were sent into exile. The Assyrians did this to all nations they conquered, thus preventing conquered nations from regrouping and rebelling against them. The Assyrians moved a lot of pagans into Galilee to replace the Jews they exiled. In Jesus' time, seven hundred years later, there were still a lot of pagans living there as well as Jews who had moved back, so the population was pretty well mixed.

The prophet Isaiah, who was living in Jerusalem at the time the Assyrians conquered Galilee, foresaw good things for that area in spite of all the devastation the Galileans suffered. Isaiah said a great light would shine upon Galilee that would bring them abundant joy. If our first reading from Isaiah sounds familiar, it's probably because we just heard it a month ago. It was part of our first reading on Christmas. St. Matthew, in today's gospel, tells us Jesus' ministry in Galilee was the fulfillment of Isaiah's prophecy. It would have been normal for a religious teacher like Jesus to do his preaching and teaching mainly in Jerusalem. (Joachim Jeremias pg 242) Jesus, however, chose to begin his ministry in Galilee. In these readings Galilee is called by the names of two of the tribes of Israel that originally settled there: Zebulun and Naphtali.

HOMILY – O'Brian was a painter, and often his bid was the lowest whenever he bid a job. That's because he thinned down his paint by putting turpentine in it. It just so happened the Church needed to be painted and O'Brian bid on the job and got it. So he got to work. After about a week of painting, there was a terrible thunderstorm and the rain came down in buckets. The paint on the church started to wash off. O'Brian was really distraught. He asked God "why?" "Why is this happening to me? What did I do?" God said this is your punishment for cheating the church. O'Brian asked God "How can I make up for what I've done?" God said: "Repaint, repaint and thin no more." Kind of a groaner, but maybe it will help you remember the message of John the Baptist and of Jesus calling people to repentance and to sin no more.

Jesus came to announce the coming of God's kingdom. John the Baptism preceded him in preparing for the kingdom. They both had the same message initially. Those who wanted to be part of God's kingdom had to change their ways (that's what "repent" means) and live a life of holiness, that is, turn their back on sin. The similarity of their message, along with other indicators, lead many scholars to conclude that Jesus worked with John the Baptist for a period of time. When John was thrown in jail because he criticized the local power, Herod Antipas, son of Herod the Great and tetrarch of Galilee, Jesus was on his own. Matthew tells us he moved on to Capernaum, a town of about 15,000 inhabitants, a place much larger than Nazareth where he grew up. Capernaum was a commercial center on a main trade route along the sea of Galilee. Naturally fishing was a local business. One could easily suspect that Jesus not only settled in Capernaum because it was a larger town, but that he also moved there to get away from his relatives and neighbors living in Nazareth. They were not very good to him. According to St. Luke's gospel, they tried to kill him.

An important word in today's gospel is the word "preach." As the gospel begins we hear: "From that time on, he began to preach: 'Repent for the Kingdom of heaven is at hand'." We come across the word again (translated as "proclaim") at the end of the gospel where Matthew tells us, "He went around all of Galilee, teaching in their synagogues, proclaiming the gospel of the kingdom, and curing every disease and illness among the people." I stress the importance of this word because it means the announcement of important news by means of a herald. The one proclaiming the message would be, for example, a delegate of the king or a magistrate. And this herald was a highly important person. If anyone dared to offend or harm the messenger, it would be treated as if such behavior were directed to the king or magistrate himself (or herself if it were a powerful woman such as Cleopatra). Jesus came representing the greatest power in all of creation, God himself.

Since we are using Matthew's gospel all this year, I might point out to you that Matthew almost always uses the phrase "kingdom of heaven" rather than "kingdom of God." It's just out of respect for the word "God." (God is not God's name; remember God gave his name to Moses. The word "God" is what God is, not who God is.) However, as we keep hearing passages from Matthew's gospel, you will notice Matthew is very careful not to use the word "God" with only three or four exceptions - a practice we might learn from, especially when we are tempted to use it profanely.

What else can we learn from today's gospel? First of all, did you notice the immediate response of the apostles? They dropped everything to join Jesus when he called. Do we ever sense Jesus calling us to stand up for our faith, witness to our faith, live our faith more seriously. How do we respond? Like the apostles? Or is our response more like: "I'll get around to it next week"? Where do we place Jesus in our list of priorities? If Jesus is the herald of the great God proclaiming the kingdom of heaven, shouldn't we listen with great attention to what he has to say?

Following today's gospel, Jesus is now prepared to proclaim his first major teaching. This lengthy instruction in Matthew's gospel is called the Sermon on the Mount. It begins with the Beatitudes which we would have heard next week - but which we won't hear, because next Sunday is the feast of the Presentation in the Temple which outranks the Sunday readings. So, until next week, let me close with a verse from psalm 95: "if today you hear his voice, harden not your hearts." Amen.

4th Sunday in Ordinary Time
February 3, 2008

HOMILY – (Zephaniah 2:3; 3:12-13, 1 Corinthians 1: 26-31, Matthew 5: 1-12a) Imagine a drug that causes you to live eight or nine years longer, make $15,000 more a year and be less likely to get divorced. "Happiness seems to be that drug," according to Martin Seligman a PhD psychologist who researches and writes about happiness. If we're miserable, can we make up our mind just to be happy as easily as if we were to take a pill? To some extent we can. Studies on twins say that about 50% of our happy or unhappy moods is genetic. About 10% depends on depressing life circumstances such as being extremely poor, gravely ill or losing a loved one. The other 40% we can control and is influenced by what we do to make ourselves happy. We just have to be careful not to pin our hopes for happiness on things like perfect health, lots of money, and good looks, which bring only a tad greater happiness than those less blessed. True happiness flows from deeper values such as engagement with family, work or a passionate pursuit, and finding meaning from some higher purpose. Does that sound like getting out of ourselves? Sitting around feeling sorry for ourselves just won't do it.

Four ideas that I think are very helpful for increasing happiness are (1) Being active (such as exercise) or (2) putting on a happy face. I think when we smile or laugh it tricks our mind into thinking we're happy and we feel happier. (3) I've always preached that gratitude is the key to happiness. Psychologists are suggesting that people keep a gratitude journal, writing down at the end of the day the things that happened that cheered them up. Experts say counting your blessings may be the single most helpful thing you can do for your happiness. (4) Doing good things for others can help too.

There are those times when a person needs professional help and/or medicine. There is that 50% that is genetic where some types of depression seems to be inherited or that 10% when a person is in a seriously difficult place in life. Self medication with alcohol or other forms of addiction only add to the problem. If you need the help, get it. There's no shame in that. A lot of depression is due to internal chemistry or external circumstances which a person can't handle on their own. For many of us the attitude we have toward life (seeing the glass as half full instead of half empty), the attitude of gratitude, of helping others, of getting out of ourselves, of surrounding ourselves with cheerful people or positive thoughts can help improve our own happiness quotient.

Then there's our faith which gives us hope. Jesus gives us the beatitudes, which form the introduction to his sermon on the mount. His sermon is three chapters long, by the way, which we will totally miss. We'll hear the very last part in June after the Lent and Easter cycle. Jesus is talking to the common people of his day, people who were living close to the edge, people under the rule of Rome, people surviving day to day. He is letting them know life's troubles and difficulties will some day be reversed for those who open their hearts to the Kingdom he came to announce. The Greek word (and Greek is the language in which we find the original form of the gospel we have) the Greek word that begins each beatitude is "μακάριος." The word means "happy" in an ordinary sense, but it also means one who is especially happy or favored or fortunate. That's why it is translated "blessed."

Reflecting on the beatitudes, it makes perfect sense to me to say that those who are poor in spirit, i.e., who are satisfied with simple things in life, those who are merciful, those who are clean of heart will be happy or blessed. It wouldn't make much sense at all to say "happy" or "blessed" are those who mourn, those who hunger or thirst for righteousness, those who are persecuted unless somehow God would remove their sadness and let them share in his joy. In that lies our faith and hope. The thing that keeps me going is to keep believing that God can bring something good out of everything. Without the happiness and hope that thought gives me, I would have given up in despair many times. Similarly I have often heard the Archbishop say during difficult times: "God's in this somewhere." I don't always see how God can make things better; I just believe he can. That's because I believe in the resurrection. If God could turn Good Friday into Easter Sunday, he can turn our sadness, our losses, our crises, our sicknesses into a blessing for us. That is the hope God gives us.

The Holy Father just finished his second encyclical: On Christian Hope. He says: our great hope – faith in Jesus – can sustain people during the roughest of times. He goes on: we need God otherwise we remain without hope. That's what brings us to Mass every week. We celebrate Jesus' death and resurrection, his body given for us and to us, and his resurrection that gives us hope that even death cannot defeat us if we stay in union with him. Blessed are we who believe in him and blessed are you for being here today. Amen.

Presentation of the Lord
February 2, 2014

INTRODUCTION – The feast of the Presentation of the Lord occurs 40 days after Christmas. In years past, today was also called the feast of the Purification of the Blessed Virgin Mary and it was called Candlemas. The last time we celebrated this feast on a weekend was 11 years ago, so the themes of the feast are most probably vague in most people's minds.

Some of you sitting in the back can see we have a stained glass window depicting the themes of today's feast. I'll try to make some sense out of it all. First the theme of the Presentation of the Lord - the official title of today's feast. This custom was based on the Old Testament Book of Exodus (chapter 13) that demanded the consecration of all firstborn males to the Lord. This law is quoted in today's gospel. This law traditionally finds its origin in that the Lord spared the life of Israelite firstborn sons when he sent the tenth plague upon the Egyptians, the plague that finally forced the pharaoh to allow the Israelites to have their freedom and leave Egypt back around 1300 BC. The original idea was that the firstborn son should spend his life serving the Lord in a special way. The parents were permitted to buy back their firstborn son from the service of the Lord for five shekels - the equivalent of about what a workman would earn in 20 days. The payment of shekels is not mentioned in Luke's gospel.

The second theme is the purification of the mother after the birth of a child. This is more complicated in that the Jews had all kinds of laws as to what was considered clean or unclean. These cleanliness laws involved certain foods, certain diseases such as leprosy, contact with a dead person or sexual activity (licit or illicit), menstruation and birth. What made a person clean or unclean was not necessarily something evil, but it was something that prohibited a person from participating in public worship until they had been purified. No one knows how certain things were classified as clean or unclean, except that the Bible designated things as such. It was an issue that led to many disagreements between Jesus and the Jewish leaders especially with regard to certain foods. In the Book of Leviticus (12,1ff), it is specified that after a woman has a boy child she must wait 40 days before she can be purified, which is done by offering a lamb and a young pigeon or a dove in sacrifice. If she cannot afford a lamb, she offers two pigeons or doves. Joseph and Mary were newlyweds and probably didn't have a lot of money. By the way, if a woman gave birth to a girl child she had to wait 80 days before she could be purified. (You figure! That was their culture and their law.)

Luke combines these two events into one ceremony at the beginning of today's gospel without going into very much detail at all. He is more interested in stressing that Joseph and Mary followed strictly the Law of the Lord and then telling us about the encounter with two holy people they met at the Temple: Simeon and Anna.

Don't worry about the length of the introduction, the homily will be short. I do need to say that the reason for the first reading is the statement of the prophet Malachi (dated about 500 years before Christ): "suddenly there will come to the Temple the Lord whom you seek." This prophecy was fulfilled when Mary and Joseph brought Jesus to the Temple.

HOMILY – I didn't explain where Candlemas fit in here. Today was the day when candles were blessed and people had processions with their candles. This connected with the words of the holy old man Simeon that Jesus was a light of revelation to the Gentiles.

The first oracle that Simeon speaks is a prayer that we say every day with Night Prayer in the Divine Office. It is a beautiful prayer expressing peace and fulfillment once God has touched our lives. For some people it's a long time of prayer and waiting before that happens as it was for Simeon and Anna. Because we do not always experience God when we would like does not mean that we should give up praying and waiting. Then we may never know him. Truth is, he is with us all the time; we just do not realize it - that's why we walk by faith, not by sight. Amen.

5th Sunday in Ordinary Time
February 9, 2014

INTRODUCTION – (Isaiah 58,7-10; I Corinthians 2,1-5; Matthew 5,13-16) Events connected with the Babylonian exile frequently appear in our Sunday readings because the exile was such an important part of Israel's history and because so many of the Old Testament writings were recorded shortly before or after that event. Those Jews who were not killed during the Babylonian destruction of Jerusalem and the surrounding territory were taken into exile into Babylon (to the area near modern day Baghdad) and they were kept in exile for 50 years. What happened in 50 years was that the Persians (the people in modern day Iran) conquered the Babylonians and allowed God's people to return home. Most of those Jews who returned to Israel were the grandchildren of the ones who were taken into exile. When they got home to Israel, they found their cities and farms in a worse state than ever. They had to rebuild everything, their farms, their homes, their businesses, their cities, their temple. Here is where our first reading comes in. Their efforts to survive created deep division in the community. The people lived by following the law of the survival of the fittest. The poor and homeless were ignored. God is telling them that their selfish, self-centered, 'every man for himself' attitude was not going to help them succeed. If they wanted to grow and thrive, they had to start caring about each other. Justice, fairness, honesty and kindness would bring light into their darkness. Selfishness would bring continued suffering.

HOMILY – We are going to be hearing mostly from the gospel according to St. Matthew this year. Matthew wrote his gospel around the year 85 A.D. His Church community was mostly made up of Jews who had become believers in Christ. Much of his material for his gospel he borrowed from St. Mark's gospel which had been written about 15 years before Matthew's gospel. There was a secondary source that he shared with St. Luke. That source was pretty much a collection of Jesus' sayings. Scholars refer to that source as "Q" which stands for the German name for source (Quelle). That source has disappeared somehow in the course of history. Matthew had some of his own material also which Mark and Luke did not have. Matthew took all of his material, that which he took from Mark, that which he shared with Luke, and what he possessed on his own and he arranged it all in a unique form. After beginning his gospel with Jesus' birth, he divides his material into ten sections. Five sections are made up of Jesus' teaching and, in-between these five sections, are stories of how people reacted to Jesus, the miracles Jesus worked, growing opposition, etc. Today's gospel is taken from the first major section of Jesus' teaching. It is called the Sermon on the Mount. This large section of Jesus' teachings (it is three chapters long) began with the Beatitudes and now, in the passage we just heard, Jesus is preparing to teach us how we are to live if we wish to be part of God's kingdom. By telling us we are salt and light, he is telling us what a major effect we can have on others and on our world if we live as he is about to show us. It is worth noting that Jesus wasn't just talking to his 12 apostles but to a large crowd. That includes us for the Scriptures are meant to teach us as well as those for whom they were originally written.

To be light for the world is obviously a positive characteristic for we all know how important light is to us. Try to imagine a world in darkness. I wouldn't want to live in such a world. No one would. During these winter days when the days are short and it's cloudy and gloomy, there are even some people who get seriously depressed simply for lack of enough sunlight. The condition is called S.A.D. (seasonal affective disorder). Jesus also tells us we are "salt of the earth." Even though we appreciate its ice melting qualities, at Jesus time salt was much more important than that. It was used as a preservative - as important to that culture as refrigeration is to us. People's food spoiled unless it had been preserved in salt.

In calling us salt and light, Jesus is praising us for he's telling us we have talents and gifts that could be of great value and of help to others, talents and gifts for which we often do not give ourselves credit. But he is also challenging us to be the gift to others that we can be. Our first reading from Isaiah describes how we can be light and salt for the world. Sometimes we are called to do big things to help others and sometimes it's the little day-to-day acts of kindness that are significant and important. Sometimes just giving another person a smile or a kind word is all we need to do - even if it is the hardest thing for us to do at that moment.

Whatever we do to help another is going to bring

blessings back to us. I'm sure we've all experienced that. I'd like to end with a quote from Patch Adams, a doctor about whom a movie was made several years ago. He is also a doctor who likes to bring humor into his healing work by playing a clown. Not humorously, however, he said this: "Hugely important is the way a person expresses thanks for being alive. The person who does so through service will possess a great comfort throughout life."

We ask the Lord to bless us today as we come before him who is the source of all light, all wisdom and all blessings. Amen.

6th Sunday in Ordinary Time
February 16, 2014

INTRODUCTION – (Sirach 15,15-20; I Corinthians 2,6-10; Matthew 5,17-37) According to the first book of the Bible, the Book of Genesis, when God created human beings he gave us instructions about what we could and could not do, and his instructions weren't all that complicated. But, according to Genesis, our first parents thought they were smarter than God and decided to make up their own rules. They found out that was a disaster. Our first reading today, from Ben Sirach, is a reflection on sin and our freedom to choose right or wrong. Some of the philosophers of Ben Sirach's time (about 180 years before Christ) were teaching that "when I sin it's God who makes me do it." The author tells us that's not so. We have a free will and are able to choose right from wrong.

HOMILY – A Sunday School teacher was discussing the Ten Commandments with her five and six year olds. After explaining the commandment to "honor thy father and thy mother," she asked, "is there a commandment that teaches us how to treat our brothers and sisters?" Without missing a beat, one little boy answered, "Thou shall not kill."

Jesus is discussing the Ten Commandments in this section from the Sermon on the Mount. Last week he told us: "You are the light of the world." Now he shows us that bringing light to others doesn't just happen. It happens only when his light fills our minds and hearts so that it can shine out from us.

Jesus begins this section by telling his audience (which includes us) that if we want to enter into God's kingdom, we have to be better people than the scribes and the Pharisees. That may not sound like a difficult task to most of us, especially with the negative impression the gospels give us of the scribes and Pharisees, but for Jesus' original audience, that probably seemed like an impossibility, because the scribes and Pharisees were looked upon as the holiest citizens in Israel. Jesus says clearly we need to be better than they were in obeying and serving God. Then Jesus gives some specific examples.

He talks about anger. This is not the anger that we suddenly feel surging up inside of us when someone hurts us or when we see someone doing wrong. Even Jesus felt that kind of anger at times. The anger Jesus is talking about is the kind of anger we refuse to let go of. Jesus talks about adultery. He makes it clear that not only is adultery wrong, but walking around with an "x" rated mind is also wrong. You may have heard the story about a guy who went to confession and had a hard time knowing what to say, so the priest tried to help him examine his conscience. At one point the priest asked "do you entertain impure thoughts?" The penitent answered, "no, they entertain me." Jesus said that's a "no, no!" Jesus talked about taking oaths. He implies there should be no need for an oath if our speech is always honest. Basically, Jesus is trying to show us holiness goes beyond external behavior. Holiness must be deep inside of us - not just an external veneer that we wear on Saturday evening or Sunday morning.

We see here too, the authority with which Jesus spoke. People were often amazed when Jesus taught and they usually remarked he speaks with authority. Certainly when he healed a sick person, or cast out a demon, he was speaking with authority. But notice how he taught in today's gospel. He said, "you have heard it was said to your ancestors," in other words, "this is what the Commandment told us," and then he adds, "but I say to you." He showed he could speak for God, interpreting what God's Commandment really meant.

I deliberately chose the short form today, because I want to address another issue. It touches on the principal that holiness is more than not just doing evil but in also doing good things. You've heard this one before about a man who died and went up to the pearly gates. Peter looked up his record and said "you didn't do anything really bad, but did you ever do anything good for anyone." The man answered "well I gave 50 cents to a beggar once." "Peter called up God and said "what shall I do with him?" God said, "give him his 50 cents back and tell him to go to hell." Well, doing good works is part of holiness. There are lots and lots of ways people can do good things for others. What I want to mention is a very diverse and at the same time specific way of doing some good. As you know, every year around this time we have the Catholic Ministries Appeal. It used to be called the Archbishop's Annual Fund Drive, but some people thought it was going to the Archbishop, so the name has been changed. The Archbishop gets none of it. It all goes to support these key Archdiocesan ministries: Catholic Charities and Social Services, the Seminary and promoting vocations, St. Rita's School for the Deaf, retired Archdiocesan priests, chaplains for colleges, hospitals and prisons. Do you want to have a little part (or a big part) in helping with all these good works? Just make a donation to the Catholic Ministries Appeal. You will get a letter about it sometime during the last week of February. Please help even a little.

Our goal is about $20,505 for this year. That's about $2000 less than the year before. So I'll tell you what, if you can give what you gave last year, we have it made. If you can give a little more, it will compensate for those who may have to cut back. Anything you give over the goal will be split with the Catholic Ministries Appeal and our own St. Vincent de Paul food pantry. Thank you for your patience and for whatever you can do. Amen.

7th Sunday in Ordinary Time
February 20, 2011

INTRODUCTION – (Leviticus 19:1-2, 17-18; 1 Corinthians 3:16-23; Matthew 5:38-48) Our first reading is from Leviticus, the third book of the Bible. It has many laws about Old Testament priesthood and Temple sacrifices, but its central message is a call to holiness for all God's people. If you look up this portion of the book of Leviticus you will see that this call to holiness includes the Ten Commandments as well as a number of other commandments – all of which are summed up in the commandment to love one's neighbor as oneself. Jesus expands on this command in today's gospel, a continuation of his Sermon on the Mount.

HOMILY – Late one night, a truck driver pulled into

a roadside café for a little something to eat. As he was eating, three nasty-looking motorcyclists noisily strutted in and made their way to the bar. For some unknown reason they gravitated toward the truck driver. One poured a little salt on his head, another knocked his pie on the floor and the third managed to knock the trucker's coffee off the counter and into the man's lap. The truck driver got up, said nothing, paid his bill and made his exit. "That dude sure wasn't much of a fighter" sneered one of the cyclists. The waiter peered out the window onto the dark parking lot and answered, "He's not much of a driver either. He just ran over three motorcycles." (Sunday Homily Helps, St. Anthony Messenger Press, for February 20, 2011) . It gives joy to our hearts to see nasty people get paid back for their nastiness. Jesus gives us a different way to look at things in today's gospel. In last week's portion of the Sermon on the Mount, we heard Jesus list several of the commandments with the phrase, "you have heard that it was said ..." and then give us his interpretation of how we were to observe them with the words, "but I say to you ..." Today's gospel continues this pattern with two other commandments: the first is the law of talion, "an eye for an eye and a tooth for a tooth." The second is the law about love of neighbor.

Let's look briefly at each of these two commandments in today's gospel. The law of talion regards proportionate recompense. It is a very ancient principle shared by all civilized people. It is a principle on which we supposedly base our own legal system in that if someone harms you, any restitution must be proportionate to the harm done. When Jesus tells us not to resist one who is evil, he is not addressing those who have responsibility to keep order in society such as law enforcement officers and judges. Their job is to vindicate the rights of the injured.

Without someone to keep order in society, there would only be chaos. Jesus is addressing the injured person himself or herself. He is not expressing it as a hard and fast rule that we have to allow ourselves to let other people walk all over us. Remember when Jesus was arrested and put on trial. When someone struck him on the cheek, he didn't turn the other cheek. He didn't retaliate either. He responded, "why did you strike me?" We are entitled to stand up for ourselves, but Jesus wants us to let love guide us rather than vengeance. If in society we always exact retribution every time we are injured or offended, we would all be going around blind and toothless as the Rev. Martin Luther King said. If all of us had to get even for every hurt in life, we would all end up hating one another. Sometimes we have to swallow our pride and move on.

Regarding the second commandment, we've all heard sermons about loving our neighbor as ourselves. This may be part of the greatest commandment but it's also one of the most difficult. There is one thing Jesus said in his comments about this command that I think is extremely practical and useful: Jesus said, "pray for those who persecute you." Some years ago someone hurt our family very badly. Whenever I thought about that person, I could feel my blood pressure go up and anger raging inside of me. One day when I was feeling very angry, these words of Jesus came to me and once they did, whenever I thought of that person, I said a little prayer for the individual. It got rid of all my anger and bitterness. I must confess that doesn't make me perfect. If that person showed up at the rectory wanting to borrow a few hundred dollars, I don't know if I would give it to them (if I had it) – I'm not that far along the road to holiness, but at least my heart is free of anger. There is a lot of benefit in forgiving. Now, when someone tells me that someone is driving them crazy or they are having difficulty forgiving, I say to them, "Jesus says pray for those who persecute you." It will bring you a lot of peace and might even surprise you by helping the other person show more kindness. Amen.

8th Sunday in Ordinary Time
February 27, 2011

INTRODUCTION – (Isaiah 49:14-15; 1 Corinthians 4:1-5; Matthew 6:24-34) The Jews certainly thought God had forgotten them after 50 years of exile in Babylon. But God tells them he hasn't forgotten. The prophet records what God spoke: "Comfort, give comfort to my people, says your God. Speak tenderly to Jerusalem and say to her that her service is at an end, (i.e. the exile is over), her guilt is expiated." (Isaiah 40:1-2) God goes on to tell his people he has written their name on the palm of his hand – an image expressing his continual remembrance of his people. Our very short first reading today is one of the most tender expressions in the Old Testament of God's love for God's people.

HOMILY – Murphy and his buddies were out playing cards one evening and Murphy was soon down $500. After he lost an additional $500 in the next hand, he grabbed his chest and fell over dead. His buddies didn't know what to do, but they knew they had to tell his wife. Sullivan was chosen to tell Murphy's wife. The other guys told him he had to be very gentle, not to shock her and to break it to her easily. He assured them he would be the essence of tactfulness. So he went to the house, knocked on the door and when Mrs. Murphy answered he told her, "Your husband just lost $1000 in a poker game and he is afraid to come home." She replied, "Tell him to drop dead." Sullivan said, "I'll be sure and do that

Mrs. Murphy." Jesus reminds us today in the gospel that we are not in control of that moment when we have to leave this world. Modern medicine may give us a little more time, but we can't avoid the inevitable. He asks us: "Can any of you by worrying add a single moment to your life-span?"

As we continue listening to the Sermon on the Mount, Jesus reminds us that entering the kingdom of heaven is more important than everything else in our lives. In a variety of ways this theme runs all through the Sermon on the Mount. In each part of the Sermon, Jesus tells us something we need to know in order to enter into the heavenly kingdom. Today's passage focuses on our everyday needs and worries.

The people Jesus was speaking to had more basic needs and worries than most of us have. Most of them were just trying to survive. Many people are just trying to survive today too, but most of us have our basic material needs met and so we worry about other things like safety and security, our loved ones, politics, health, the price of gas, whether I should get a new cell phone, worrying whether my nose is too big, keeping up with the Jones', etc. As important as some of our concerns are, God's kingdom is more important. Jesus tells us, "Put God first and have more trust in God."

We must not distort his message like the boy who wrote home from college: "Dear Mom and Dad, today's gospel reading was all about not worrying over things like food and clothing because God is going to give them to us anyway, and it takes our minds away from what really matters. That gave me a whole new perspective. From now on, I'm not going to worry about getting good grades, finding a job, etc. God knows that I need them and God will come through. Your loving son. P.S. In case God is slow getting around to me, I need $800.

(from Preaching Resource, CelebrationPublications.org, Feb 27, 2011, pg 4)

God expects us to use our brains to deal with life and to provide for ourselves. There is a line in George Bernard Shaw's play Joan of Arc. Joan was discussing with her general whether she should go into battle with an army that vastly outnumbered her own. She said God would help her win. Her general told her, "God is no man's daily drudgery." The general as it turned out was right. Joan lost the battle. God is not going to do for us what we should do for ourselves. He's not going to do our laundry, pay our bills, cut our grass or plant our gardens. We have to do for ourselves what God gave us the power to do.

There are those times when we are not in control. That's when we must trust in God's love and care. If we don't trust, we can worry ourselves to death, but Jesus doesn't want us to do that. There is a line from St. Paul that is very helpful to me. He tells us, "for those who love God, all things work out for the best." (Rom 8:28) Believing that brings me a lot of peace. Amen.

1st Sunday of Lent
March 9, 2014

INTRODUCTION – (Genesis 2,7-9; 3,1-7; Romans 5,12-19;Matthew 4,1-11) Today's first reading tells us the story of the creation of our first parents, their temptation and their fall from grace. The story is more theological than it is historical. It tells us God created the human race to be happy and to share in his grace and friendship. This is symbolized by the Garden of Eden where our first parents had all their needs met. But things didn't turn out as well as God intended. This story presents one explanation for the problem of evil in the world, a problem that St. Paul attempts to explain in today's second reading. In these passages we are told that evil finds its source in our decision to give in to temptation, in our attempt to make our own rules and to use our free will to say "no" to God. In the gospel, Jesus, who has come to save us from evil, has shown us how to resist temptation.

HOMILY – A wife noticed on her husband's workbench a broken vise. Being a very thoughtful person, she decided to buy him a new one for his birthday. She went to the hardware store and asked the salesman, "Do you have any heavy-duty vices?" "Sorry," he replied. "I gave them all up for Lent." (Reader's Digest: Laughter, the Best Medicine, pg. 286)

Getting rid of some of our vices, whether heavy-duty or not, is what the Church is trying to get us to do as we begin this holy season. We have just heard two stories from the Bible: a story about Adam and Eve and a story about the temptations of Jesus. Let me begin by talking about our first parents. Science tells us the first modern humans appeared to have lived about 200,000 years ago and this Scripture passage was written around 3,000 years ago. Since no one was probably around to record what was happening 200,000 years ago, the important message here is not a historical description of the beginning of human life but the theology it teaches us. Behind this story is the concept that God has the authority to tell us what we must do and not do. It is a concept that a greater and greater part of our culture seem to ignore as they create their own rules about what is right and wrong, sinful or not. Our first reading also gives us a typical picture of temptation. Like Adam and Eve, we often find ourselves attracted to something God said we must not have or do, and we become convinced God is just trying to keep us from being happy or fulfilled. The story of Adam and Eve is the story of all of us. Temptation is an illusion, and giving in to it may please us for a moment, but it does not really bring us any lasting happiness. Usually it leads to problems. It certainly affects our relationship with our own conscience (if it's in good working order) and it affects our relationship with God and not in a positive way.

This leads us into the gospel reading about Jesus who showed us that temptation can be overcome with the help of God's word. Matthew, Mark and Luke tell us in their gospels that after Jesus was baptized and the Spirit came upon him, the Spirit drove him into the desert where he remained for forty days and was tempted by Satan. It's Matthew and Luke who describe Jesus' temptations for us. They are certainly different than the run of the mill temptations most of us have to deal with. Jesus' temptations dealt with if and what kind of Son of God he was. Remember that at Jesus' baptism, God the Father spoke about Jesus: that Jesus was his Beloved Son, with whom he was well pleased. So in the temptations, Satan challenged Jesus: "if you are the Son of God, change these stones into bread" or "if you are the Son of God, throw yourself down from the top of the Temple. Nothing is going to hurt you." The temptations also dealt with his Messianic calling. Satan in effect was saying, "use your special powers to satisfy your hunger, or to get attention from the Jews and their leaders when you come floating down from the top of the Temple, or make yourself powerful over the whole world by adoring me." It is most likely that Jesus was not tempted in exactly this way in the desert, but that he faced actual temptations such as these in the course of his ministry. One example: after Jesus miraculously fed 5,000 people with five loaves of bread and two fish, everyone in the crowd wanted to make him their king. He refused their attempt to elevate him to that position, but I'll bet he might have wondered whether he could have had greater influence over many more people if he allowed them to make him their leader and their king. One temptation I'm sure he went through was during his agony in the garden right before his death. Before Judas showed up with the soldiers, he could easily have walked away from it all, given up preaching and healing and just live a quiet life until he died a peaceful death. But he would not walk away from his ongoing mission of teaching and healing and trying to destroy the power of Satan.

What does all this mean for us? It shows the kind of Messiah Jesus would be, humble, faithful, here to serve and not be served, and ready to pay whatever price this would require of him. It shows what kind of Son of God he was, that he loved the Father with his whole heart and soul and mind and strength. It shows that no matter how holy we are and how filled with the Spirit of God, we still have to guard against the temptations of the devil, for he is interested in leading any one of us astray. He goes about like a roaring lion looking for someone to devour. (I Peter 5,8) It shows that because Jesus experienced temptation, he knows how hard it is to resist and he understands us when we give in to it and is greatly pleased with us when we succeed in resisting it. And he wants us to know that he will help us when we are tempted and he encourages us not to let Satan get the better of us. May this Lent give you greater strength to resist temptation. Amen.

2nd Sunday of Lent
March 16, 2014

INTRODUCTION – (Genesis, 12,1-4; II Timothy 1,8b-10; Matthew 17,1-9) Our first reading takes us back almost 4000 years to the time of Abraham. His name was Abram before God gave him a vocation and a new name. Abram came from an ancient civilization known as Sumer, a settlement near modern day Kuwait. He and his family migrated to the northern part of Syria, near Turkey. After a lengthy stay there, Abram heard God's call to leave his kinfolk behind and move to the land of Canaan - modern day Israel. To make this move, he had to leave behind a prosperous commercial area to settle in a land that was still relatively primitive and undeveloped. Abraham made this long and difficult journey at the tender age of 75 along with his wife, Sarah, who was 10 years younger. God was telling them, not only to pack up and move to an unknown territory, but to start a family there as well! It was a pure act of faith on the part of Abraham to follow God's call and to believe in the blessings God kept promising him, promises we hear in today's first reading. In the gospel, we have the account of the Transfiguration, which was a promise of Jesus' future glory in the resurrection and future glory for those who follow him faithfully.

HOMILY – Three words begin today's gospel: "after six days." (Luke says eight days - but who's going to argue over such a small detail). Those three words are not printed in your books but they are in the Bible. We hardly ever hear a reference to time in the gospels. The miracles and teachings that make up Jesus' ministry just seem to follow one after the other without any specific indication as to what order they occurred in or how they were connected. Here, however, Matthew, Mark and Luke want us to know that the transfiguration of Jesus is necessarily connected with some previous event. That event was when Jesus asked his disciples "who do you say that I am?" I'm sure you remember that very important passage. Peter answered correctly as we know, when he said "you are the Christ." (i.e. the Messiah) But when Jesus began to teach them he would have to suffer greatly, they balked at that idea. Peter's resistance to Jesus' teaching about suffering earned him the strongest rebuke to ever come from Jesus when Jesus said to Peter: "Get behind me, Satan!" Jesus then went on to warn the apostles they would have to suffer too: "If anyone would come after me, let him deny himself, take up his cross and follow me."

It was within a few days that Jesus was transfigured before Peter, James and John. At that very moment, the apostles could really see Jesus: as Christ or the Messiah AND as he will be in risen glory. They would not have such an opportunity to see Jesus again in glory until after Jesus' resurrection, so Jesus told them not to speak to anyone about the vision until Jesus was raised from the dead. I guess if they did tell any of the others about what they had experienced, the others would have thought they had lost their minds.

The main emphasis here is on Jesus, the one about whom God the Father said: "listen to him." As Jesus had earlier told all the apostles, "If anyone would come after me, let him deny himself, take up his cross and follow me," so there is here in Jesus' transfiguration a message of hope for those who follow him, hope that someday his followers would share in his glory since they have shared in his cross.

It is about these words of God the Father, "listen to him," that I want to say a few words. If we listen to Jesus and follow him perfectly, we would never need to say, "I'm sorry." We wouldn't need to have a season of Lent calling us to repent, to change our ways, to pray and fast and give alms. We wouldn't need to have such a thing as the sacrament of confession or reconciliation.

Usually we have a Penance Service during Advent

and Lent. This year, however, our Archbishop asked all the parishes in the Archdiocese to open their doors to make available the sacrament of confession. That's what is happening on Tuesday of this week. We will be open on Tuesday evening from 7:00 to 9:00. Fr. Lammeier and I will be hearing confessions. If it's not a very busy evening, I'll just hear them alone. If you would rather go to another priest, most other parishes will be open for confessions at the same time.

I consider hearing confessions one of the most privileged parts of my ministry. It's as if I could be like Jesus and say to a person who could not walk, arise and walk, so in confession, assuring a person of God's forgiveness and love is bringing them peace and setting them free. Sin and guilt are psychologically and emotionally crippling and forgiveness is freeing.

Can't a person go directly to God? Yes, but signs are helpful in connecting us with God. I can talk to God on my own, but if a voice came out of the heavens to say to me "you are forgiven, I love you as my child," that would be even more reassuring. The priest's voice, "I forgive you your sins," is that voice from the heavens assuring us of God's forgiveness. It is exactly what Jesus said to the apostles on Easter Sunday night: "Peace be with you." Then he breathed on them and said, "receive the Holy Spirit, whose sins you forgive, they are forgiven them, whose sins you retain, they are retained." Of all the things Jesus might have said when he first appeared to his apostles, the power to forgive sins was one of the most important things he wanted them to be able to do. They would be continuing Jesus' work of offering his love and forgiveness of people.

I can almost visibly see the peace that forgiveness can bring, and that's why confession is such a privileged part of my ministry as a priest. It's a great miracle to be able to speak the words of forgiveness. Sometimes I feel blessed to be able to offer a person some good advice. This Tuesday evening from 7:00 to 9:00. We'll keep the lights on for you. Amen.

3rd Sunday of Lent
March 23, 2014

INTRODUCTION – (Exodus 17,3-7; Romans 5,1-2.5-8; John 4,5-42) In our first reading, we hear of an event that takes place as Moses is leading God's people through the desert to the Promised Land. It was probably two or three months since they left Egypt. Twice the Bible tells us God had provided, in a miraculous way, food and water for them. Once again they are demanding water for themselves, their children and their livestock. Moses sounds desperate as to what to do. When he turns to God, God takes care of their needs. God was not going to abandon them now after he had taken them this far. The reading prepares us for the gospel when we hear Jesus offer "living water" to a woman he meets in Samaria as he is traveling in that area. She misunderstands the term "living water" until Jesus explains it to her. This living water that leads to eternal life he offers to us today as we meet him in faith and prayer.

HOMILY – An ad in the local newspaper read: "For sale, sleeveless wedding gown, white, size 8, veil included. Worn once, by mistake." Was the woman in Samaria, who had had five husbands, a person who made lots of mistakes or a woman who had buried five husbands? John doesn't tell us, and Jesus wasn't ready to tell her she needed to get her life in order. He was interested in bringing her from where she was to a deeper relationship with God. So he starts off with a simple request, asking for a drink of ordinary water. One of the things that is unusual about this whole gospel is that Samaritans hated Jews and vice-versa. They would never use one another's cups or dishes. And men never talked with women in public. Another thing that is unusual about the gospel is that Jesus met her at the well in the middle of the day. In that culture it was customary for the women to come to the well early in the morning. Quite possibly the woman in the gospel was looked down upon or maybe spoken to as if she were some kind of low life by the other more righteous women in the village and she was trying to avoid them. But ignoring all these cultural taboos, Jesus simply asks for a cool drink of plain water. John doesn't tell us if he got the drink of water because before she knew it, Jesus was talking with her on a purely spiritual level, offering her living water, like a spring of water welling up to eternal life. It's interesting when we analyze this encounter - how Jesus could take a simple, ordinary object or idea and move it to a higher spiritual level. We saw how he did it with the request for a drink of water. The subject then changes when the woman talks about where a person should worship God, whether on Mt. Gerizim (a mountain near Jacob's well) or in Jerusalem. Jesus says the day will come when it won't matter about what mountain we choose to worship on but that we will worship the Father in Spirit and truth. Jesus does the same thing with ordinary food. When the apostles bring him some and encourage him to eat, he tells them there are more important things in life than having something to eat - as important as that is. Jesus tells his apostles that doing God's will nourishes us at a more profound and more lasting level of our being. Lastly, Jesus comments that's it's almost time for the harvest, only to point out the spiritual harvest that is about to happen as he sees all the village people (people hungering for the word of life) coming down the road to meet him. Jesus also changed this woman, from someone who was most likely seen as a sinner, into a preacher of the gospel when she announced to the town's folks about this special man she had met. Notice how John subtly reveals who Jesus is. In offering living water, he was claiming to be greater than the patriarch, Jacob. The woman came to discover Jesus was a prophet because he could see exactly what kind of person she was. He admitted to being more than a prophet when he said he was the Messiah - a rare admission in the gospels, especially among Matthew, Mark and Luke. Lastly, the town's people who came to meet him acclaims Jesus as the Savior of the world.

Today in the gospel we meet a woman, a woman who most likely had the reputation of being a sinful person. Jesus was often criticized for associating with sinners, but that didn't keep him from reaching out to her for a simple favor - all the while being aware that he wanted to do a favor for her. Little did she know what that one day in her life would be like. In the middle of the day, she went out to get some water from the town well as she most likely did every day and, before she knew it, she was recruited as an apostle, announcing to her whole town about this outstanding person she met and inviting the people to come to meet him. Life is that way for all of us sometimes. We never know what is around the corner. Let's pray that it's always something good waiting for us and if it is the Lord we encounter it will be good. We just have to be a bit careful how involved we want to be with him. He has shown how he can capture us completely: heart, soul, mind and strength. He may ask us for a glass of water and before we know it we are preaching the gospel to all our neighbors, friends and relatives. Amen.

4th Sunday of Lent
March 30, 2014

INTRODUCTION – (1 Samuel 16: 1b,6-7,10-13a; Ephesians 5: 8-14; John 9: 1-41)Our first reading takes us back 1000 years before Christ. At that time Israel was being ruled by King Saul, Israel's first king. Saul had not pleased God, so God sent Samuel, his prophet, to anoint someone else who would be the future king after Saul died. That king would be David, son of Jesse from Bethlehem. All of Jesse's sons had the dignity and physical characteristics of potentially good leaders, but the judgment Samuel had to make could not be guided by what he saw with his eyes. He had to see with his mind and heart under the inspiration of God's Spirit. This reading from the Book of Samuel prepares us for the gospel where Jesus healed a man who was born blind by giving him the ability to see with his eyes. The man gradually came to see with his mind and heart who Jesus really was. He is contrasted with the Jewish leaders who had eyes to see, but who were blinded in their hearts by jealousy, pride and arrogance.

HOMILY – **A** pastor of a non-Catholic church had to be fitted for a set of dentures. The following Sunday he preached for only 5 minutes. The Sunday after that he preached about 7 minutes. The third Sunday, he preached for one and a half hours. His parishioners asked him what was going on. He said for two weeks his teeth hurt him so much after seeing the dentist that he could talk for just a few minutes. But on the third Sunday he accidentally picked up his wife's false teeth and couldn't stop talking. (This doesn't apply to any of the wonderful women I know.)Today's gospel is one of my favorite readings, but it is long. So don't worry, for that reason I'm not going to talk for a long time.

I want to first of all point out an important lesson at the beginning of today's gospel. It is a lesson on suffering - it makes clear to us that suffering is part of being human and is not necessarily a punishment for sin. Sometimes our sinful ways bring us suffering, but all suffering cannot be traced back to some sin we had committed. My grandmother was a very holy person, but in her later years she became bed ridden and she always thought God was punishing her for something she did. Jesus said the man's blindness was not due to any evil thing he or his parents had done. It was just part of the human condition.

Now, let's get to the point of the gospel. The point is that Jesus is the light of the world. He gave sight to the blind, but more than that, he gives light to our minds and hearts - light that guides us through life to eternal life. If we do not follow his light, we will be like the Pharisees who could see with their eyes but were blind in their minds and hearts. As the old saying goes: "there are none so blind as those that will not see." (Matthew Henry)

I want you to notice the gradual insight the blind man developed about Jesus. The first time he spoke of Jesus, he said "the man called Jesus anointed my eyes." Then when the Pharisees questioned him about Jesus, the man said, "He is a prophet." He has to have come from God or he would not be able to do anything. Lastly, when Jesus asked if he believed in Jesus as the Son of Man, the man said, "I do believe" and he worshipped him." A practical lesson here is that believing and worshipping go together. Too many people today are willing to say "I believe" but they seldom have time to worship. The day of the Lord is filled with everything else but time for the Lord.

Although we may not be blind like the Pharisees, if

we were we wouldn't be here, sometimes we are like the parents of the man born blind in that we hesitate to talk about what we believe because our friends may not like us or think less of us. Notice how the parents of the man born blind wouldn't say anything when they were questioned. They just said: "talk to my son, he's old enough to speak for himself."

Let us pray that we continue to come to know Christ as our light, and not to be intimidated by anyone because we believe in him. Amen

5th Sunday of Lent
April 6, 2014

INTRODUCTION – (Ezekiel 37: 12-14; Romans 8: 8-11; John 11: 1-45) first reading comes from about 600 years before Christ during the Babylonian exile. The prophet Ezekiel, who was in Babylon with the other Jewish exiles, had a vision of a field covered with dry bones. The field of dry bones represented God's people and their nation which was destroyed by the Babylonians. In his vision Ezekiel saw God join these bones together, cover them with flesh and breathe life into them. It was a prophetic vision that God would bring his exiled people back to their homes and to their land. Today's first reading concludes and interprets Ezekiel's vision of the dry bones. This reading emphasizes for us that God is the source of life and it prepares us for today's gospel which is about Jesus raising his friend Lazarus from the dead.

HOMILY – We just heard John tell us of the last and greatest of Jesus' signs. The first half of John's gospel tells us of many signs Jesus worked: signs of his love, his power, his saving mission such as changing water into wine, healing the royal official's son, healing the paralyzed man at the pool of Bethesda, the multiplication of the loaves and fishes, walking on water and healing the man born blind which we heard last Sunday. These signs were carefully arranged by John to build up the one we just heard today, his last and greatest sign. Notice, John does not refer to these acts of supernatural power as miracles but as signs, because they all have a special significance; they indicate for us why Jesus came. Today's sign shows us most clearly why he came. As Jesus tells us in John's tenth chapter: "I came that they may have life, and may have it to the full." (Jn. 10,10)

Ironically, in raising his friend Lazarus back to life, Jesus is unleashing the fury of the religious leaders in Jerusalem. How did that happen? It's because many more people started to believe in Jesus after Jesus raised Lazarus back to life and the Jewish leaders grew more determined to get rid of Jesus. They also planned to kill Lazarus if they could. As a sign, today's miracle pointed into the past to encompass the other signs that tell us who Jesus was and why he came, but it also points into the future. The raising of Lazarus pointed to Jesus' own resurrection. There was a big difference between Lazarus' being raised back to life and Jesus' resurrection. Lazarus was raised back to the life he originally enjoyed; Jesus was raised to eternal glory. Lazarus would die again; Jesus would never die. So Lazarus came out of the tomb still wearing his burial garments, because he would need them again; when Jesus rose, he left his burial cloths in the tomb. He would not need them again.

I've told this story before. When I was in the Holy Land about 24 years ago, we visited all the places that were important in the gospels: Bethlehem, Nazareth, Capernaum, the Sea of Galilee, Mt. Tabor, Jerusalem, Gethsemane, Calvary - all of which were impressive and moving for me, but the most moving part of my travels was the tomb of Lazarus. I stood in the empty tomb, a small room which had been carved out of the rock with one little light bulb hanging down from the ceiling, and such a great sense of awe came over me. These words of Jesus from today's gospel penetrated my whole being: "I am the resurrection and the life. Whoever believes in me, even if he dies, will live, and everyone who lives and believes in me will never die." Overwhelmed, I thought: "whoever in the history of the world could ever make the tombs empty, and here I am, his disciple and his friend." After Jesus spoke these words of self-identification: "I am the resurrection and the life," he asked Martha: "do you believe this?" He also asks us that same question today. "Do you believe this?" (say "yes!") Of course you do. Otherwise why are you here? Amen.

Palm Sunday of the Passion of the Lord
March 13, 2014

HOMILY – Does anyone know what a kinkajou is? I came across this word for the first time this week and I had to look it up in a dictionary. A kinkajou is about the size of a large raccoon. It is related to the raccoon family and can be found in the wild in southern Mexico, Central America and the northern parts of South America. It has a strong tail it can use to hang from a tree limb; it has sharp claws and sharp teeth. A lady in Florida decided she wanted one for a pet. Having a dog was too commonplace, but having a pet kinkajou was really cool. It was a cute little pet when it was small, but when it experienced puberty for the first time, it went berserk. It tried to eat its own tail and tried to tear itself to pieces. The family was bitten and scratched trying to save the little creature from destroying itself. (from National Geographic, April 2014, pg 118). You might be wondering why the family would subject themselves to getting bitten and clawed to save this little animal? The answer (and it's an important answer) is this. It was a wild animal and its nature showed itself at this mature stage of life. The nature of this family who loved their pet also showed itself in their efforts to save it from destroying itself. The nature of the wild animal conflicted with the nature of the caring family.

We just heard the story of Jesus giving his life for us. Many times I've been asked, "why did Jesus have to die?" The reason goes back to the fact that it was in his nature to save us and he could not stop doing everything he was trying to do to lead us to salvation. There are elements in our nature that are driven by selfishness, pride, jealousy, cruelty and all kinds of attitudes and behaviors that work against God's desire to save us. In Jesus' passion we saw intense and pure love on the part of Jesus (that was his nature to be that way) and we saw the dark side of human nature working against him and trying to destroy him.

Because it is in Jesus' nature to love, he continues to reach out to us in love. He speaks to us each week in the Scriptures, he nourishes us each week by feeding us with his own body and blood. He willingly shares his Spirit with us so that we can continue to live and love more like he does as we stumble along making our way to eternal happiness. Amen. (thoughts from National Catholic Reporter 3/28 to 4/10/2014, pg 27)

Holy Thursday
March 20, 2008

HOMILY – (Exodus 12:1-8, 11-14; 1 Corithians 11: 23-26; John 13:1-15) When Jews gather for the Passover, which is described in the first reading, the youngest child asks: "why is this night different from all other nights?" The head of the family answered the question by describing how God saved his people from slavery and brought them to the Promised Land. The more I thought about tonight and how I would answer the question "why is this night different from all other nights" the more ideas came to mind. Don't worry, I'm not going to try to put all that could be said into my homily tonight. As a matter of fact, we could spend the rest of our lives reflecting on the central elements of our faith that we celebrate tonight and still not exhaust all the meaning they contain.

So I want to reflect on the virtue of faith as it is demanded by the Eucharist, and the virtue of love as it is demonstrated in the washing of feet. I think the Eucharist is the greatest test of our faith for Catholics today. It is a test I believe the statistics on Mass attendance show is too much for many Catholics to cope with. It challenges our minds to accept that the Son of God, who took on human flesh, could just as easily take on the form of bread and wine and become our food and drink. In tonight's gospel Peter could not imagine that their master and Lord would stoop to wash their feet. Jesus said "you don't understand it now, but you will understand it later." Peter's response was "you'll never wash my feet." Jesus said "unless I wash you, you will have no inheritance with me." In other words Jesus said to Peter: you just have to believe me that what I am doing for you will keep us united throughout eternity (what else could Jesus have meant by his inheritance).

These words are amazingly similar to what Jesus said earlier in John's gospel about the Eucharist: "unless you eat the flesh of the son of man and drink his blood you do not have life within you." Peter had to simply take Jesus on his word even if what Jesus was doing didn't make sense to him. In the Eucharist we have to simply take Jesus on his word, "this is my body," even if what Jesus says doesn't make sense to us.

Scientists tell us today there are certain foods that nourish us and certain foods that are of little value or that can even be harmful to us. The foods that truly nourish us do so, not because they look or taste wonderful, but because of certain invisible nutrients in the food. So when Jesus said, "the bread that I will give is my flesh for the life of the world," if we believe him to be trustworthy, then we will trust that there is something in this food that will give us eternal life – we don't know how. Paul tells us that tonight in the second reading which is the oldest written account of the Eucharist. As I said at the beginning, I could contemplate this for the rest of my life and still probably would not understand. But as Jesus said: "you will understand later."

The second main idea this evening's liturgy focuses on is love and service. Have you ever wondered why we have the gospel of the washing of the feet tonight and not focus entirely on the Eucharist? I think the reason is that the Church wants us to know that love and service is as important as the Eucharist, for without love, as Paul said: "I am nothing." Since actions speak louder than words, Jesus gave us an example in action to help us remember how important it is. The washing of feet was the task of a servant for who would enjoy washing feet when people had to walk dusty, dirty roads where animals as well as humans walked? But Jesus' act of humility in washing the apostles' feet was only a preview of his great act of humility in giving his life for us on the cross. Lest we forget this act of love and service, he asked us to "do it in remembrance of me." Notice in the reading from Paul Jesus says this twice because it's so important – so important that we not forget. "Why is this night different from all other nights?" When this question was answered at the Passover supper with the description of God saving his people, the answer helped the youngest child (and everyone else at the dinner) to gain a sense of their identity as God's people. When we gather here tonight we are given, through the liturgy, a sense of our identity as God's people, followers of Jesus Christ who gather here in faith to celebrate his memory, to receive him as our food and drink and to love one another.

Good Friday
April 18, 2014

HOMILY – (Isaiah 52:13–53:12, Hebrews 4:14-16; 5:7-9, John 18:1–19:42) The first part of today's homily is taken from a homily by St. Aelred, an abbot who was famous as an outstanding preacher in England, Scotland and Ireland in the 12th century. St. Aelred says: One of the most radical and difficult things Jesus asks of his followers is to Love your enemies, and pray for those who persecute you. Anyone can love the person who loves them. The perfection of love lies in the love of one's enemies. Jesus not only told us to do this but he gave us an example. We read in Luke's gospel how Jesus prayed for those who were putting him to death: "Father, forgive them, they know not what they do." (Lk. 23,34) Think of this, people spat on him, blindfolded him, scourged his, crowned him with thorns, mocked and made fun of him and in the end nailed him to the cross and while remaining gentle, meek and full of peace he prayed: "Father, forgive them." Is any gentleness, any love, lacking in this prayer? Yet, it was not enough for him to pray for them, he wanted also to make excuses for them: "for they know not what they do." They are great sinners, yes, but they do not see what they are doing; therefore, "Father, forgive them." They are nailing me to a cross, but they do not know whom they are persecuting and killing: "if they had known they would never have crucified the Lord of glory;" (I Cor. 2,8) therefore, "Father, forgive them." They think it is a lawbreaker, an impostor claiming to be God, a seducer of the people. I have hidden my face from them, and they do not recognize my glory; therefore, "Father, forgive them, for they do not know what they do." St. Aelred asks: How can we love with a heart like Jesus? We must keep the eyes of our inner self always fixed on the serene patience and love of our divine Lord and Savior.

I have a couple of thoughts I wish to add to St. Aelred's sermon. When Jesus uses the word "love," he's not talking about warm, fuzzy feelings. He's talking about having in us an effective desire for a person's well-being. That means not holding grudges and hatred in our hearts toward anyone. By effective, I mean a willingness to help a person who might need our help.

The second thing I want to add is that love for our enemies does not mean we have to let them walk all over us. We are allowed to stand up for ourselves. Remember when the servant of the high priest struck Jesus, Jesus didn't say, "here's my other cheek, you can hit me there too." He said, "why did you strike me?" Tell me what I did to deserve that. At other times he confronted the Jewish leaders with their rudeness to him and with their plotting to kill him. Even though he confronted them, he didn't try to retaliate or get even with them. A few times he even walked away when the Jews wanted to kill him. He could have walked away this time too, when Judas betrayed him. Notice how they all fell to the ground when Jesus said "I am" the mysterious name for God. But in God's plan this was the time for Jesus to give in, the time for him to lay down his life so that he could take it up again. (Jn. 10,17) And in taking it up again, he would draw all people to himself (Jn. 12,32) and make us sharers in his victory and in his new life. That hope of overcoming the power of death and sharing in Christ's glory is one of the reasons why we celebrate Easter and why we call today GOOD Friday. Amen.

The first half of this homily are thoughts from the reading for the liturgy of the Hours for the Friday of the first week of Lent - a homily by St. Aelred, abbot.

Easter
April 20, 2014

HOMILY – St. Matthew, in his gospel, tells us that a rich man, Joseph of Arimathea, a secret follower of Jesus, asked for Jesus' body when Jesus died. He buried Jesus in his own new tomb. Some clever person added this comment to Matthew's account: one of Joseph's friends asked him why he would give up his new tomb to this penniless preacher, who was just executed as a criminal. Joseph's answer was "not to worry. It's just for the weekend."

I want to say a few things about the empty tomb, because the empty tomb is one of the proofs of the resurrection. Even though Jesus predicted he would rise from the dead, no one really expected it to happen. It took a lot of convincing and appearing to the apostles to convince even his closest followers. Joseph of Arimathea would never have made such a remark that Jesus would need the tomb "just for the weekend."

That tomb is still empty; Joseph was never buried in it nor was anyone else. The early followers of Jesus continued to have immense reverence for Jesus' tomb and the early Christians, even almost three hundred years later, remembered where Jesus had been buried. What is impressive is 100 years after Jesus died, the Roman emperor Hadrian filled in the entire area and built a pagan temple, with a special shrine to Venus over the spot. It was almost 200 years after that when Constantine tore down the temple, excavated the area and found the tomb just where the Christians told him it would be. Today the Church of the Holy Sepulcher is built over the tomb of Jesus.

The third thing about the tomb, according to Matthew, is that Pilate allowed the Jews to station guards at the tomb. Whether or not the guards saw Jesus rise, we do not know, but when the angel rolled back the stone that sealed the tomb, the guards were greatly frightened by the angel. The angel came to open the tomb, not so Jesus could come out, but that people could see in, to know that Jesus was no longer there, that he had risen. St. John tells us Jesus left behind the burial clothes; he would never need them again. The burial cloth that is honored as the Shroud of Turin is controversial, but I am convinced it is genuine.

Another proof of Jesus' resurrection are all the appearances of Jesus to his disciples and his friends. St. Paul gives us a whole list of people who saw and spoke with Jesus. Paul doesn't mention any of the women Jesus appeared to because women did not have the legal standing of being able to be a witness. However, Jesus did not hesitate to make some of his women followers witnesses to his resurrection. When he appeared to them he told them to tell the apostles that he had risen. Mary Magdalene especially is frequently referred to as the apostle to the apostles. It wasn't just the witness of those who saw Jesus that convinces me that Jesus had really risen. It was that these witnesses were willing to die for what they said they had experienced. That's the important thing for me; no one is going to die for something they know is not true.

One more thing gives me confidence about the resurrection. It is an event Luke describes in the Acts of the Apostles. When the Jewish leaders were trying to keep the apostles from preaching about Jesus, the Jewish leaders were arguing about what might be effective. A Pharisee named Gamaliel proposed this argument: he said lots of other people have claimed to be the Messiah, but when they died, their followers dispersed. So if this Jesus is a fake, this whole movement will fall apart; however, if this Jesus is for real, we'll never stop people from following him or preaching about him, for we would be fighting against God himself. All we need to do is to look around the world today and see all the people who believe in Jesus to know that Gamaliel was right and Jesus is for real. (Acts of the Apostles, 5,34ff).

Personally, my belief in the resurrection of Jesus is my source of strength. I know he is with me in prayer, in the sacraments, in the work that I do, and I know he is with those I love who have moved on to the next life. I hear they now have a movie about the book Heaven is for Real. I read the book a few months ago and enjoyed it. I'm looking forward to seeing the movie. It fits in pretty well with other things I've read about near-death experiences.

I wish you all a deep faith in the resurrection of Jesus.

It will be a source of strength for you, and I pray all of us one day may enjoy eternity in his kingdom. Amen.

Second Sunday of Easter
April 27, 2014

INTRODUCTION – (Acts 2,42-47; I Peter 1,3-9; John 20,19-31) In our first reading today, St. Luke gives us a lovely picture of the early Church - how it was one big happy family where everyone was agreeable with one another and cared about each other. If we read a little further in the Acts of the Apostles, we see this idyllic condition didn't last very long. Some members cheated on their socialistic system as persecutions came and as the Church kept growing. With almost one and one-third billion Catholics in the world today, we can hardly expect perfect harmony, but we remain united by four basic elements that St. Luke identifies for us in today's first reading: (1) holding to the teachings of the apostles, (2) to the communal life (trying to help one another to some degree - even if not totally sharing all our possessions), (3) celebration of the breaking of bread (their term for the Eucharist or the Lord's Supper) and (4) to prayer. This statement tells us that being a member of the Church is more than just a matter of saying we are a Catholic or having our name on some Church's roster. St. James' famous statement: "Faith without works is dead," is another way of saying that an inactive believer is not a believer at all. (James 2,17)

HOMILY – We have an expression in the English language that characterizes the event John tells us about in today's gospel, "a doubting Thomas." Poor Thomas, he gets reviled because he seems to be lacking in faith. Well, Thomas did have faith; he was the one who spoke up when Jesus decided to go to Jerusalem and the other disciples tried to dissuade him from going. They said to him: "Rabbi, the Jews were but now seeking to stone you, and are you going there again?" It was Thomas who said: "Let us also go, that we may die with him." (Jn. 11,16).

Let me make one more reference to what is commonly viewed as Thomas' lack of faith. Actually, Thomas was not asking for anything that hadn't already been given to the other apostles. Easter Sunday they all saw Jesus; they saw his hands where the nails had been and the wound in his side that was large enough for a person to put their hand inside. Whether any of them touched him or not, we don't know, and we don't know whether Thomas touched him either. He just wanted the same opportunity the other apostles had. Once he was given that opportunity, he expressed one of the most profound acts of faith found in the Bible: "my Lord and my God." It was an expression of faith that sprang not so much from what he saw with his eyes, but what he saw with his mind and heart. It's an expression of faith that many people say in their own mind and heart when they see the priest raise the host and chalice at the consecration or when they are preparing to receive communion.

Why was it necessary for all the apostles (including Thomas) to see the risen Christ? Because they would be his witnesses to the world that Jesus had truly risen. That's the job Jesus gave them to do. As he told them before his ascension: "you shall be my witnesses in Jerusalem and in all Judea and Samaria and to the end of the earth." (Acts 1,8) We have also been called to be witnesses even though we have not seen the risen Jesus; we are witnesses to our faith in Jesus, witnesses to the peace our faith gives us, the guidance, the sense of God's presence and God's love; we witness by our kindness, our honesty, our willingness to serve, our charity to the Church and to the poor, the time we take to pray, our forgiveness of those who have hurt us. In other words, people should be able to see God at work in us by the way we live.

I have a few other thoughts I need to mention. I want you to notice the first words Jesus spoke to the apostles: "peace be with you." Immediately he followed this up with breathing his spirit upon them and giving them the power to forgive sins. When we're struggling with the power of sin in our lives, we are not at peace. It is extremely significant that the first thing Jesus wants his apostles to do is to forgive sin. Sin, of course, gets in the way of our relationship with God, and Jesus came to help us be one with God. It is because we read about Jesus giving the apostles the power to forgive sin that this Sunday has been designated Divine Mercy Sunday. You don't have to wait for Divine Mercy Sunday every year to ask for God's mercy and forgiveness. That is always available to us when we approach Jesus asking for his mercy. So if you fall into a sinful state, don't wait until next year this time to come for forgiveness. Get it done right away so you can enjoy the peace only God can give.

Today cannot go by without mentioning that our Holy Father, Pope Francis, is canonizing two holy men tomorrow: John XXIII who started an aggiornamento, a bringing the church up to date. Probably what we most are grateful for is that he allowed the Mass to be cele-brated in the vernacular, in the language we are familiar with. Many people think John was chosen because of his age (77) and after the almost 20 year reign of Pius XII, it seemed to many that this old man would give the Church a chance to sit back and relax for a couple of years. He really surprised everyone. Actually, John was chosen for his positive qualities, his exemplary piety, his loyalty to Pius XII whom he did not always agree with, his fluent use of many languages, his talent for conciliation and his immense experience of diplomacy. He narrowly helped avert a war during the Cuban missile crisis He served the Church faithfully and wisely and with joy for about 4 1/2 years.

The second man being canonized is John Paul II, noted for his long reign (26.5 years), the first non-Italian pope for 455 years, an athlete, a brilliant and prolific writer and teacher, a pope who liked to show his interest and concern to all parts of the world by his 104 "apostolic voyages." He liked giving recognition to hundreds of people (482) to be exact from all over the world for their holiness by naming them saints - holy people who have lived their faith in an outstanding way. He helped weaken the hold Communism held on the world. His dedication to God and to the Church is unquestionable.

Jesus said "blessed are those who have not seen and have believed." That is most of us including popes and saints. We don't have to see Jesus to be blessed or holy. We simply have to believe in him and live as he has taught us and as we saw in our first reading: that means adhering to the teachings of the apostles, caring for and helping one another, participation in the sacraments and prayer. Amen.

Third Sunday of Easter
May 4, 2014

INTRODUCTION – (Acts 5: 27-32, 40b-41; Revelation 5: 11-14; John 21: 1-19)In our first reading we hear Peter's first sermon - the one he gave on that first Pentecost. This is the same Peter who just a few weeks prior to this speech denied he even knew Jesus. Now, filled with the Spirit of God that had just been sent upon the disciples, he speaks out boldly about Jesus - that God raised our Lord back to life after he had been put to death and that Jesus is now exalted at God's right hand as Messiah and Savior.

HOMILY – Did you ever feel really, really discouraged? Maybe you wanted to walk away from Church and never come back because you felt as if God let you down. Or you wanted to run away from home because of angry words or a member of your family was really mean to you. Maybe you decided you were going to quit your job or quit school because you felt you were treated so unfairly. We've all had those experiences. Maybe we have actually walked away. Wouldn't it be interesting if a stranger started walking along with you, gave you a chance to talk about what you were feeling, and then explained why things happened as they did? You begin to see things more clearly. You invite the stranger to stop along the way for something to eat. Bread usually shows up on the table first; the stranger takes the bread, says a blessing, breaks the bread, then hands you a piece. Suddenly you realize it is Jesus you are talking to. He smiles and then disappears. He doesn't say goodbye, he doesn't get up and leave. It's as if he is still there but he can no longer be seen.

In today's gospel St. Luke tells us of two disciples who had put all their hopes in Jesus and when Jesus was put to death, they thought it was all torn away from them. They had heard that Jesus had risen, but they didn't believe it. Jesus' conversation with them and the breaking of the bread made them realize Jesus really was alive; their hopes returned.

Can you imagine anything like this happening to

yourself or to anyone else? St. Luke, in today's gospel, is telling us it happens all the time, especially when we come to Mass. Jesus does not desert us in our disappointments and discouragements. "I am with you always," he told his disciples before he ascended to the Father. But we do not recognize him. He might come as a stranger; he might speak to us through a book we're reading or through a friend or just in the quiet of our hearts. He especially speaks to us through his Word in the Scriptures. He nourishes us and blesses us in many ways. Too frequently we forget about the many ways he blesses us because all we can think about are the things that worry us or bother us. Especially he nourishes us in the Eucharist. We do not know whether Jesus celebrated a Eucharist for these two disciples when they sat down at a table to eat - but St. Luke wants us to think of the gift of the Eucharist when he describes what Jesus did as he sat at table with the two disciples. Notice the words: "he took bread, said the blessing, broke it and gave it to them." It is the exact same way St. Luke described what Jesus did at the Last Supper when he changed bread and wine into his own body and blood.

Today we have four of our second graders who are making their first Communion. We congratulate them and their parents as they move forward in their journey to grow closer to our Lord. May we meet our Lord each week in the Eucharist and grow in our love for him. And may we always know that the Lord is with us, helping us along life's path. Even though we do not see him, he assured us he is with us and we believe in him.

Fourth Sunday of Easter
May 11, 2014

INTRODUCTION – (Acts 2,14a.36-41; I Peter 2,20b-25; John 10,1-10) Pentecost is the setting for our first reading. After the Holy Spirit came down upon Jesus' first followers, the Apostles left the upper room where they were gathered and started speaking in a variety of languages so that people from all over the Mediterranean world, who were in Jerusalem that day, could understand them in their native language. For those who were wondering what was going on, Peter gave an explanation. Today's reading is the conclusion of Peter's sermon. He proclaims Jesus is Lord and Christ; i.e., as Lord, Jesus is divine and as Christ, Jesus is the Messiah, the savior of God's people. In the second reading from the first letter of Peter, the saving mission of Jesus is proclaimed, so that we, like lost sheep, could be brought back to God.

HOMILY – Happy Mother's Day to all mothers and to those who fill in as mothers in helping children to become mature adults. I apologize for an excess of humor today. It will make up for the times when I couldn't find a good joke. A clever writer, in writing about mothers, proposed the idea that mothers are the same the world over. And to support this assertion, she speculated that mothers of famous people would probably have said the same thing to their children that mothers do today. Such as: PAUL REVERE'S MOTHER: "I don't care where you think you have to go, young man, midnight is past your curfew." MONA LISA'S MOTHER: "After all that money your father and I spent on braces, that's the biggest smile you can give us?" COLUMBUS' MOTHER: "I don't care what you've discovered, you still could have written." MICHELANGELO'S

MOTHER: "Can't you paint on walls like other children? Do you have any idea how hard it is to get that stuff off the ceiling?" NAPOLEON'S MOTHER: "All right, if you aren't hiding your report card inside your jacket, take you hand out of there and show me." ABRAHAM LINCOLN'S MOTHER: "What's with the stovepipe hat? Can't you just wear a baseball cap like the other kids?" ALBERT EINSTEIN'S MOTHER: "But it's your senior picture. Can't you do something about your hair?" GEORGE WASHINGTON'S MOTHER: "The next time I catch you throwing money across the Potomac, you can kiss your allowance goodbye." JONAH'S MOTHER: "That's an interesting story. Now tell me where you've really been for the last three days." THOMAS EDISON'S MOTHER: "Of course I'm proud that you invented the electric light bulb. Now turn it off and get to bed." (The Joyful Noiseletter, Dec. 2002, pg 1)

I know you came here for something more than entertainment, even though humor is good for one's spirit. You have come to be strengthened and guided and loved by the strength and wisdom contained only in the power of God's word. But before we get to today's scriptures, on this Mother's Day we cannot forget to say a prayer to Mary, God's Mother and our Mother. We had our May crowning on Friday and we left the statue of Mary here to remind us that Mary will always be our Mother who deserves our honor and who will hear our prayers.

In today's gospel, we hear Jesus talking to us about shepherds. He uses very simple examples that his hearers would understand. Sheep were a major part of Israel's economy and they still are. The examples Jesus uses are easy enough for us to understand even if we've never been any closer to sheep than having to put on a woolen sweater on a cold day. Jesus approaches the ideas he wants to communicate from several aspects. Today's first parable compares Jesus to the shepherd whose voice the sheep recognize and whom they follow. Each of us is important to him as he tells us the shepherd calls each by name. The image sort of reminds us of the one lost sheep out of a flock of 100 and the shepherd leaves the 99 in the wilderness to go looking for his lost sheep. (Luke 15, 3-7) He loves each of us personally and he calls us to follow him. In the second part of today's reading, Jesus compares himself to the gate into the sheepfold. Others have tried to get in, such as some of the Jewish leaders, but they unfortunately were motivated by power and pride. Jesus' way is the only way - as he said at the Last Supper: "I am the way and the truth and the life; no one comes to the Father except through me." (John 14,6)

The most important verse for me in today's reading goes like this: Jesus said: "I came so that they might have life and have it abundantly." (John 10,10) We all experience losses and disappointments in this life, no matter who we are, rich or poor, young or old. We seek to find fulfillment; sometimes we succeed; sometimes we do not. Here in this verse, Jesus gives us the promise of the fullness of life. Just knowing ourselves to be one with him introduces us to that more abundant life. In the end, what God has planned for us is beyond our comprehension. From what I've read about people who have had a near-death experience and who find themselves lifted into heaven's glory, they usually do not want to come back to this life. After that experience they no longer are afraid to die - especially as life goes on and we lose friends, physical and mental abilities, and many things we took for granted in our youth. We have to keep remembering Jesus is our life, that he is the way and the truth and the life. Amen.

Fifth Sunday of Easter
May 18, 2014

INTRODUCTION – (Acts 6, 1-7; I Peter 2, 4-9; John 14, 1-12) Three weeks ago we heard St. Luke tell us in the Acts of the Apostles how the first Christians got along so harmoniously. Luke tells us they devoted themselves to prayer and instruction from the Apostles and generously shared their material possessions so that no one was in need among them. As the community of believers grew, so did the problems. The very first believers in Jesus were Jews from around Jerusalem who spoke Hebrew or Aramaic. Soon Jews from other countries around the Mediterranean came to believe in Jesus. Like good Jews, they would come back to Jerusalem from time to time. For the most part they spoke Greek, the common language of the Roman Empire. They tended to be more partial to Greek customs and ideas than the Jerusalem Jews. Because they spoke Greek, they were called Hellenists. When the Hellenists came to Jerusalem, they felt as if they were being treated like second-class citizens, especially when food was being handed out. Remember, in those days widows were entirely dependent on the community for their basic needs (sort of a welfare system). The Hellenists complained that their widows were being overlooked and not getting their fair share. The Apostles felt their role was not to distribute food but to stay focused on prayer and preaching. They solved the problem by creating a new office in the Church, the diaconate. I am so grateful the Apostles did that then and that the Second Vatican Council has restored the permanent diaconate. Wherever I've been, I've always had great deacons to help in the ministry of the parish.

HOMILY – I want to start with a story. The story goes

that after the Spirit came on Pentecost, the Apostles divided up the different regions of the world, and by chance, Thomas was chosen to go to India. Although he didn't want to go, Jesus appeared and persuaded him to go. Thomas had been a carpenter in his younger years. When he got to India, he met the king who was intent on building a palace for himself. Thomas discussed the project with the king and the king was convinced Thomas would do a great job of building a beautiful palace. So the king gave Thomas a large sum of money and went on a trip. Thomas took all the money and gave it to the poor and never started building the palace. After a while the king sent a messenger to ask Thomas how the palace was going and Thomas said it was coming along fine. He just needed some more money for the roof. So the king sent more money and Thomas again gave it all to the poor and did not even start on the palace. Shortly thereafter, the king figured the palace must be almost finished, and being eager to see it, decided to come back home. When the king found out Thomas had given away all the money the king had given him and had done nothing on the palace, he had Thomas arrested and decided to have him put to death. It just so happened, while Thomas was in prison, the king's brother, Gad, dies. Gad's spirit was taken to heaven and an angel showed Gad a number of wonderful mansions he could choose from for his eternal dwelling place. As Gad was considering which mansion to choose, he saw an exceptionally beautiful mansion on a lovely estate and decided he wanted that one. The angel said "no," that particular mansion was the palace Thomas has been building for the king. All the good works Thomas did with the king's money which was distributed to the poor went into building that wonderful mansion. Gad said he had to tell his brother, the king, before the king put Thomas to death. So Gad was allowed to return to earth for a short time to tell his brother, the king, about the mansion in heaven. Gad promised his brother a blessed afterlife if he became a follower of Jesus, which he did. My story comes from a writing called the Acts of Thomas that goes back to about 100 years after the time of the Apostles. The story is imaginative and non-historical - more like a parable.

When I reflected on today's gospel, the image of a beautiful palace or mansion kept coming to me. Jesus said: "in my Father's house there are many dwelling places. I am going off to prepare a place for you." Jesus' words are very comforting when we think of death, whether it is our own or the death of someone we love. Today's gospel comes from Jesus' discourse at the Last Supper. He knew how traumatic it would be for his Apostles when he was put to death and he told them not to let their hearts be troubled. That would be almost an impossible challenge for them, but Jesus gives them the means by which they could avoid great distress: he said have faith. "You have faith in God, have faith also in me."

Jesus said he is going to prepare a place, but we must not forget we are preparing the place, too, by our good works. Jesus said in the Sermon on the Mount: "Enter by the narrow gate; for the gate is wide and the way is easy that leads to destruction, and those who enter by it are many. For the gate is narrow and the way is hard, that leads to life, and those who find it are few." (Mt. 7,13-14) Also, the Book of Revelation reminds us that when we leave this world our "good deeds go with" us. (Rev.14,13) Our gospel reminds us that at present we are living in two worlds. We have our everyday world of keeping a roof over our head and putting food on the table, and we have a world which we hope to be part of forever, a world where Jesus (together with us) is building a place for us to be able to enjoy our heavenly Father, his presence and his love, and the love of all our brothers and sisters, for all eternity. Amen.

Sixth Sunday of Easter
May 25, 2014

INTRODUCTION – (Acts, 8,5-8.14-17; I Peter 3,15-18; John 14,15-21) St. Luke's Acts of the Apostles tells us how the message of Christ spread throughout the Mediterranean world, starting at Jerusalem. The power behind this growth was the Holy Spirit and the risen (yet invisible) presence of our Lord. As the ministry grew, the Apostolic leaders needed more helpers and so last week we heard how they chose seven other men who were ordained to serve, men we now call deacons. Initially they helped with the daily distribution of food to the poor and widows, but it wasn't long before they were preaching the gospel of Christ. The first martyr was one of these seven, St. Steven. He spoke with such power that the enemies of Christ could not debate with him; they could only destroy him. Another one of the deacons, Philip, whose name we hear in today's first reading, was the first to announce the good news of the resurrection of Jesus in Samaria. The Samaritans were hostile to the Jews and vice versa, but the gospel was well received there. The Apostles 'confirm' the ministry of Philip with an even greater outpouring of the gifts of the Holy Spirit.

HOMILY – Tom figured out a way to remember his wife's birthday and their wedding anniversary. He opened an account with a florist and told him to send flowers to his wife on those dates, along with a note signed, "Your loving husband." His wife was thrilled by the attention, and all was great until one anniversary, Tom came home, saw the bouquet, kissed his wife, and said, "Nice flowers. Where'd you get them?" You can't put love on cruise control or automatic pilot. Relationships take an ongoing involvement of ourselves, even in our relationship with God.

In the Garden of Eden, Eve asks Adam: "Do you love me?" Adam answers: "Of course, Eve! You're my one and only love." Adam was smart enough to give the right answer. With God we're often tempted to let other things take a higher priority in our lives than God, such things as sports, pleasure, money, our own ego, etc. (both jokes from Reader's Digest, Laughter Really Is the Best Medicine, pg 62 and 81)

In today's very short gospel reading Jesus uses the word "love" five times. In our culture today that word "love" conjures up images of romantic love. Now romantic love is good. Without it the human race would have become extinct a long time ago. But in our culture it's overdone; it's the kind of love that's most written about, portrayed in movies and soap operas, etc. Sometimes people feel their religion is not satisfying them because when they pray or when they hear Jesus teach us we should love God, they say I don't feel anything, I don't feel close to God, I don't feel thrilled to go to Mass on Sunday. I don't know what's wrong with me. What's wrong is they are thinking in the context of romantic love. When Jesus speaks of love he has a different meaning. He is not speaking of the kind of love that our modern day culti Greek, and in Greek, there are three different words for love. There is a word for romantic love (eros) and a word for friendship love (philia) and a third word, one used most often in the Scriptures, is agape which means esteem, affection, a giving and caring kind of interest in another.

When Jesus speaks of love in today's passage, he is speaking of agape love. It is characterized not so much by the kind of feelings it gives us, which are sometimes warm and affectionate, full of gratitude and peace, having a sense of God's presence, but sometimes our feelings are feelings of doubt, darkness, emptiness, which are experiences even saints have. We can't measure our love for God by our feelings. But Jesus does give us a way of knowing whether we love God: "If you love me you will keep my commandments," he tells us. This is a reality that is true in all our relationships. When we love others with an agape love, we are willing to go out of our way for them, be concerned about them, spend time with them; if they need our help we're willing to help. We even treat our pets this way; we care about them and care for them.

Today's gospel setting is at the Last Supper. Jesus is preparing to leave his apostles, but he asks for their continued love even though he would no longer be visible to them. He is not deserting them; he is not leaving them orphans. The Holy Spirit will be with them; the Holy Spirit will allow them to know that This love is conditioned, not on God's part, for God always loves us, but it is conditioned on our part, for if we say we love God but are not keeping his commandments, we are placing ourselves at a distance from God and from the true love for God, agape love, which will lead us to a peace and joy we will never know in this world, and it will be forever. Amen.

Feast of the Ascension
June 1, 2014

HOMILY –(Acts 1:1-11; Ephesians 1:17-23; Matthew 28,16-20) Many of you know the story of how St. Boniface Church began. Since, however, 2013 is the 150th anniversary of its founding and we have been celebrating that anniversary for the past year, I thought it would be appropriate to say a few words about our history. Catholics who settled in this area of Cumminsville, as it was called, went to St. James Church in White Oak or traveled downtown to a Catholic Church down there. By the way, the name Northside was used to designate the north side of Cumminsville. In 1853 a parish was established in Northside and was named St. Aloysius. Within just a few years, the parish had grown so large that a second parish was built. The official reason for this was they needed more space to accommodate everyone. The unofficial reason, I have heard, was that the Irish and the Germans who made up the congregation didn't get along with one another very well. They drew lots as to who would keep St. Aloysius, and the Irish won the draw. The Germans were given $1500 to build a new church. That's a bit more than what the parish will have to pay to put a new garage door on my garage. The German church was dedicated in November, 1863, and appropriately named St. Boniface after the patron saint of Germany. St. Aloysius Church's name was changed to St. Patrick, the patron saint of Ireland. I might mention that my great, great uncle, Fr. Boniface Godfrey Topmoeller was the second pastor of St. Boniface and he pastored the parish for 21 years. Of course, I can't go into detail about everything that happened here in the past 150 years, but I would like to mention a couple of personal items. Over

100 years ago my grandparents built their home just one block away on Delaney St. where they lived for the rest of their lives. My mother, aunt and uncles all went to St. Boniface School and my parents were married here. They were German. My father was Irish, so after their marriage they went to St. Patrick's and that's where I went to school for three years. Twenty- five years ago, I was stationed in Loveland, and when I left there, I was so worn out that I requested a year and a half sabbatical, which the Archbishop allowed. When it was time to come back to work in a parish, I was sent to St. Patrick's and was told that I should work to merge St. Patrick's and St. Boniface. Within a year they were merged and now the Northside community, which began as one parish, is one parish again and I have been blessed to be the pastor here for almost 23 years. That's almost half of my priesthood. A lot of people's lives have been touched here at St. Boniface. The time has really gone fast. That's the end of my history lesson. I am grateful to all those who worked hard making it possible for us to celebrate 150 years.

Today we celebrate the Ascension. It is interesting that our gospel from Matthew does not mention the Ascension. Matthew's gospel ends with an appearance of Jesus after the resurrection. What Jesus had to say on that occasion, which I will reflect on in a few moments, is appropriate to today's feast. First I want to say a word about how Mark, Luke and John deal with the Ascension. John only mentions the Ascension in Jesus' comments to Mary Magdalene when he appeared to her. Mark has a very brief mention of it, without giving any detailed or visual description of it. The image we all have of the Ascension comes from both the gospel of Luke and the Acts of the Apostles which Luke also wrote. Luke gives us two versions of the Ascension. In his gospel he tells us Jesus ascended on Easter Sunday night and in the Acts of the Apostles, Luke informs us that Jesus ascended 40 days after Easter. Fr. Benoit makes a useful distinction between these two portrayals in Luke's two volumes. The ascension of Jesus on Easter can be understood as the glorification of Jesus in his Father's presence; i.e., being seated at God's right hand thus making the ascension an essential part of the resurrection while the levitation of Jesus' body 40 days later symbolized the terminus of the appearances of the risen Jesus. During that brief period of time between the two ascensions, Jesus made many appearances: to his women followers, to his apostles and to other disciples, instructing them and assuring them he had truly risen. (Ray Brown, The Anchor Bible, John XIII-XXI, pg 1012)

This brings us back to today's gospel. It is an appearance of the risen and glorified Jesus. If we accept Fr. Benoit's explanation of Jesus' ascension to glory on Easter and his other ascension 40 days later, Jesus would already be seated at the right hand of the Father in this appearance to the eleven in Galilee which we just heard in today's gospel. Indeed we could assume that from what Jesus said in the gospel: "All power in heaven and on earth has been given to me." Today's gospel is often referred to as the Great Commission. Matthew stresses the teaching part of Jesus' ministry as he commissions the eleven to carry on his teaching mission. They are to teach all nations what Jesus taught them and baptize them, and they are to know that Jesus is still with them. Matthew begins his gospel with this theme when he quotes Isaiah the prophet that "the virgin will be with child and bear a son, and they will call his name 'Emmanuel' (which means 'God with us')." Matthew now ends his gospel on that note.

And on that note I will continue on with the Mass, knowing that Jesus is always with us, but especially when we are united with him in the Eucharist. Amen.

Seventh Sunday of Easter
May 16, 1999

HOMILY – (Acts 1:12-14, 1 Pet 4:13-16, John 17:1-11a) Jesus was asked one time what is the most important commandment in the law. We know how he answered. He not only gave us the most important commandment but the second most important commandment as well, two commands that perfectly compliment each other: to love God with our whole heart and soul and mind and strength and to love our neighbor as ourselves. Jesus gave us the answer not only by his words but also by the way he lived.

I would like to reflect today on how Jesus showed love for his Father. His perfect obedience was one way he showed his love. Another way he showed it was by spending time with his Father in prayer. That is what we especially want to focus on today. The topic of prayer was inspired by today's gospel which is part of Jesus prayer at the Last Supper. We have little or no information about what his life was like before he began his public ministry. The little information we do have shows us that Joseph and Mary were faithful in their Jewish observances. Thus Jesus would have been brought up in that tradition, going to synagogue on the Sabbath and going to the Temple in Jerusalem annually for Passover. St. Luke tells us that when Jesus was beginning his ministry he went to Nazareth and went to the synagogue on the Sabbath "according to his custom."

Synagogue services would have been very similar to

the first part of our Mass. There would be common prayer and readings from the Law and the prophets and with a commentary after each reading. St. Luke points out in his gospel that Jesus was praying as John the Baptist baptized him. Immediately after that, recall how Jesus went into the desert for 40 days to fast and pray. His encounter with the devil there showed he knew the scriptures well and he could quote them easily. Frequently it is mentioned that during his public ministry Jesus was at the Temple participating in liturgical celebrations there. The gospels tell us about Jesus getting up early in the morning to pray or staying up all night in prayer. He would spend time in prayer before important decisions or important events. One time after seeing Jesus praying, the disciples asked him to teach them to pray and of course we are all familiar with the prayer he taught them. In addition to the Our Father, Jesus taught a lot about prayer. For example the parable of a man who had a friend visit him at night and he went to his neighbor to borrow some food, and he kept on knocking until he got what he needed. That's the way Jesus said we should pray. Even when he wasn't teaching about prayer, his teachings reflect the deep relationship Jesus had with his Father. There is no doubt about it, prayer played a major role in Jesus life. The Last Supper of course was more than an ordinary supper. It was the Passover which Jesus was celebrating with his disciples, which was a religious celebration.

His prayer (in the 17th chapter of John) is divided into three parts. First Jesus prays for himself, then for his apostles, then for all who would come to believe in him. Notice how many times the word "glory" is used in today's gospel. Jesus saw his death and resurrection as a moment of glory, a moment when God's saving love would be revealed to the world. He prays that the Father might be glorified in all that was to take place and that in the fulfillment of his mission, he might be a source of life for all who would believe in him. It is comforting to know he prayed for all of us at the Last Supper. He continues to intercede for us each time we celebrate the Lord's Supper.

There is not the time to analyze this prayer thoroughly. My main point today was simply to point out the prayerfulness of Jesus. We see in the first reading how Jesus followers imitated his example as they gathered together in prayer in the upper room after the Ascension, waiting for the coming of the Holy Spirit. Louis Evely in his book, Teach us to Pray, wrote: "Too many Christians regard God as pilots regard their parachute, namely, good if needed, but better if they can get along without it." We might wonder why would Jesus need to pray? He was already as close to the Father as he possibly could be. I am sure there are many reasons why Jesus prayed, but this question might best be answered with another question: "why do we need to spend time with those who are important to us, with those whom we love?" A true disciple of our Lord will make prayer a priority in their lives, and by "prayer" I mean more than just a rapidly recited Our Father or Hail Mary. Prayer is spending time with our God. Do we feel like we're too busy? I will never forget what our spiritual director in the seminary told us. The busier we are the more we need to pray.

Today we come together for the greatest prayer there is. As we gather in prayer today, we are not alone and I don't mean simply that there are others here in church with us. Christ is with us and it is in union with his perfect sacrifice of love and obedience on the cross that we offer our prayers and praise to God our Father.

Vigil of Pentecost
June 8, 2014

INTRODUCTION – There are eleven possible readings for the feast of Pentecost, six for the vigil and five for the feast itself. [On Sunday there is a special sequence before the gospel. Only Easter and Pentecost have a special sequence that is required and Corpus Christi has an optional one.] That's because today is indeed a special feast, the third most important feast in the Church year. That's why I asked everyone to wear red, the color of the Holy Spirit. Today's feast celebrates the completion of Jesus' saving work with his sending of the Holy Spirit.

Our first reading today is from Genesis. The story follows the story of the great flood. Those who survived the flood intended to make sure they would be able to escape floods in the future, so they decided to build a high tower. Notice a little satire here. In their pride, they are going to build a tower up to the heavens and God decides to "come down" to see what's going on. He confuses their speech to put an end to their prideful building project. God does not want to divide people but to unite them. In the account of Pentecost, in a passage that is read Sunday from the Acts of the Apostles, that's exactly what he does as he gives the apostles a special gift of tongues so that people from every nation would understand the message of God's universal love that they were preaching.

Pentecost
June 8, 2014

HOMILY – Most of our prayers to the Holy Spirit involve asking the Holy Spirit to come. A monk named Symeon, the New Theologian who lived about 1000 years ago, wrote a prayer that begins: "Come, true light! Come, eternal life! Come, hidden mystery! Come, nameless treasure!" It goes on and on using thirty different titles for the Holy Spirit, each of which starts with the word "come." (I Believe in the Holy Spirit, Congar, Part II, pg 112) [The sequence we just prayed follows a similar format.] Two weeks ago, we heard a gospel where Jesus was talking to his apostles at the Last Supper. He told them "I will not leave you orphans; I will come to you. In a little while the world will no longer see me, but you will see me because I live and you will live." "I will ask the Father, and he will give you another Advocate to be with you always, the Spirit of truth." It is this other Advocate who gives us the hope and the joy and the love that comes from knowing that Jesus is with us. Just as Jesus reveals the Father to us, the Spirit reveals Jesus to us. Especially do we experience this in the Sacraments, in helping a person in need, and while reading the Scriptures. St. Augustine speaks of the Spirit as our inner Master, our inner teacher, or as Jesus calls the Spirit, the Spirit of truth.

I could give many examples of how the Spirit has touched my life, but I will limit it to one. I may have told this story before, and if I have, please pardon me for repeating it. When I was in grade school, the Sisters encouraged all of us to say three Hail Mary's every day that God would help us know what our calling in life was to be, whether we would serve God as a married person or dedicate ourselves to a religious vocation, whether we would be a teacher or book keeper or secretary or sales person. So from grade school on, for many years I said three Hail Mary's every day, never sure what I should be. I thought of being a farmer or an artist or an accountant or teacher. The one thing on my list I kept hoping

I wasn't being called to do was to be a priest, because, as a priest, I knew I would not be able to marry and have a family. Because the idea kept coming back to me, I decided maybe that's what God wanted, so I decided to go to the seminary after Elder. I had a lot of doubts as to whether it was right for me, but I promised myself I would try out the seminary for one year. The next year I went, still full of doubts, and I committed myself only for one year. I did that for about five years until one day I was in the chapel praying, and all of a sudden, in an instant, every doubt left me. It was like I had been in a dark room and someone came along and turned on all the lights. Being the compulsive type that I am, I had to check to see if what I felt was for real. I stopped asking God if he would show me what he wanted me to do, and I prayed that if being a priest was something he didn't want me to do, he would have me flunk out of the seminary. That was the only sign I asked for. God gave me a sign I didn't ask for: my grades significantly improved after that experience. I guess that was like Pentecost for me. It was an experience that kept me from dropping out of the priesthood in the 60's and early 70's, while other priests were requesting laicization. I saw guys leave the priesthood who were much more talented, much more intelligent, much more personable than I was and I asked myself, what do they see that I don't see that they are leaving. But the experience I had in the chapel that day in the seminary continued to make clear to me where God wanted me.

The Spirit is like the wind; we can't see the wind but we can see what it does as it shakes the trees and flies the kites and brings in the clouds that give us rain. The Spirit works in hundreds and thousands of ways, to be a gift to us and to help bring us to God. When people tell me they are not religious but they are "spiritual" I hope it is the Holy Spirit that is guiding them and not a narcissistic spirit. There are many kinds of spirits and some of them are not the kind we want to follow. St. Paul tells us: "when the Holy Spirit controls our lives, the Spirit will produce in us: love, joy peace, patience, kindness, goodness, faithfulness, gentleness and self-control." (Galatians 5,22-23). It's no wonder we pray Come, Holy Spirit, Come.

Feast of the Holy Trinity
June 15, 2014

INTRODUCTION – (Exodus 34,4b-6.8-9; II Corinth 13,11-13; John 3,16-18) Today in our first reading we hear about Moses who lived about 1300 years before Christ. At that time and for hundreds of years thereafter, all the nations that surrounded Israel worshipped many gods. It would be difficult to count all the Egyptian, Greek or Roman gods, some of which we are familiar with, but imagine having 700 gods to keep track of. Evidence was discovered that around the time of Abraham (about 4000 years ago), the Babylonians did honor 700 gods. If a person had to pray to all of them, they would never get to eat or sleep. Since the gods expected earth people to give them honor and sacrifices, one would become anxious thinking one or the other god might come and take vengeance on you for neglecting to give him or her appropriate worship! Anyway, that's the way it was for centuries - except for the Hebrews. Their God revealed to them that there was no other God, but their God, often called the God of our Fathers or the Holy One of Israel. In the early history of the Hebrew people, they believed there were other gods in the world, such as the gods of the Egyptians, the

Babylonians, or the Canaanites, but their God was the only God they must worship. We know from their history they failed a lot in limiting their worship only to their own God. Around 500 or 600 years before Christ, they came to the conclusion that the gods of other nations did not exist at all, that their God was the only God in the entire world and their God was powerful everywhere. At the time of Moses in 1300 BC, when God was leading his people out of Egypt, God gave them a special gift: he told them his name. Having God's name symbolized a more intimate relationship between God and his chosen people and it meant also they could call on God, by name, when they needed God's help. In our reading today, we hear God revealing his sacred name to Moses. In the Hebrew bible, that name is Yahweh, but the Jews chose never to pronounce it. That is because they wished to avoid any possible risk of saying God's name in vain. So whenever Yahweh came up in the sacred text, as it does today, they always substituted the word "Lord." God not only revealed God's name but God revealed the kind of God he was: God is merciful and gracious, slow to anger and rich in kindness and fidelity. Although God has no gender, it tends to be customary to refer to God as "he" because Jesus taught us to think of God and pray to God as our Father.

HOMILY – Congratulations and best wishes to all of our fathers and father figures. We are all grateful for your support, your guidance and direction, your patience, your dedication and most of all your unselfish love.

We inherited our faith in one God from the Jews. When Jesus came, an observant Jew, he revealed to us new ideas about this one God. Jesus spoke of God as Father, yet Jesus showed himself to be God. He healed people, raised the dead, forgave sins and gave the apostles the authority to forgive sins, he cast our demons, he interpreted the Torah (the law of God) with authority, and he spoke not as if he were the Father, but as if he were equal to the Father. In John's gospel he says: "I and the Father are one," and "he who sees me sees also the Father." He tells the Jews "before Abraham was, I am." (Abraham lived 1800 or 1900 years before Christ). He prays for himself: "Father, glorify me in thy own presence with the glory which I had with thee before the world began." He prays for his apostles, "I pray that they all may be one; even as you, Father, are in me, and I am in you." In addition to what Jesus said, and by showing signs that he was divine, Jesus spoke of the Holy Spirit as the Spirit of Truth, another Advocate who was neither Father nor Jesus, who would speak with authority, and would take what belongs to Jesus and declare it to the apostles.

How to integrate all this with faith in one God took a few centuries as Church Fathers debated, as various heresies arose, as wars were fought and blood was shed especially in the long process of overcoming the heresy of Arianism, which taught that Jesus was not equal to the Father. Eventually a Church Council, the Council of Nicaea in 325, declared what we profess each Sunday in the Nicene Creed, that the Father is God, the Son is God, the Holy Spirit is God; the Father, however, is not the Son and the Son is not the Father and the Father and Son are not the Holy Spirit. The council of Nicaea did not say much about the Holy Spirit, so more was added on to the Creed by the council of Constantinople in 381. The difficulty of dealing with the mystery of the Trinity continues today as the Church suffered centuries ago and continues to suffer a great split in what it believes about the Holy Spirit. Roman Catholics teach the Holy Spirit proceeded from the Father and the Son while Orthodox Christians say the Holy Spirit proceeded from the Father through the Son. And still today two of the largest denominations of Christians in the world are the Roman Catholic Church and the Orthodox Church.

Should we be surprised that God is too great for us to fully understand? If we perfectly understood what God is like: we would be as great as God. We just accept what is a mystery, the mystery of the Trinity, a term given to us by Tertullian around the year 200 AD.

Why should the Trinity matter? Simply because God wants to reveal God's self to us, just as two lovers want to share with each other their hopes and dreams and joys and fears. God wants us to know him as well as is possible because he loves us and wants us to love him. The Trinity also matters because it is the only way that we can know the greatness of Jesus and the love Jesus has for us that our God humbled himself totally for our sake. The persons of the Trinity are united in love, and God is a model for how he would want us to be, not fighting with one another or exploiting one another but loving and caring about each other.

Let me sum this all up with two quotes I thought were very good. The doctrine of the Trinity is given to us in Scripture, not in formulated definition, but in fragmentary allusions. Alister McGrath said about the Trinity: the individuality of the persons is maintained while each person shares in the life of the other two.

The Body and Blood of Christ
June 22, 2014

INTRODUCTION – (Deuteronomy 8,2-3.14b-16a; I Cor. 10,16-17; John 6,51-58) The setting for our first reading is on the east side of the Jordan River across from the Promised Land. Moses' job of leading the people of God is just about finished. He is giving them some last minute instructions before they cross the Jordan and enter the Land and he goes off to his eternal reward. His fear is that the people, once they get comfortable in this new land, will become complacent and forget the God on whom they depend. So he tells them to remember - remember the journey from Egypt, remember the long time they spent in the desert and especially remember the food with which God fed them - the manna. This reading (especially the mention of manna) is meant to introduce us to the main focus of today's feast - how God sustains us with the flesh and blood of his Son, Jesus, the bread of life.

HOMILY – Food is a big part of our lives. Not only are we aware of it throughout the day (and even at night sometimes), our newspapers, magazines, books, ads on TV keep telling us about food, how to fix it, where to buy it, what tastes good, what is healthy for us and what isn't.

When Jesus taught, he used examples that touched the lives of the simple people in the culture in which he lived. I suspect their interest in food was just as great as ours. The whole sixth chapter of John is about food. It begins with Jesus feeding a crowd of 5000 people with 5 barley loaves and two fish. None of the gospel stories tell us how he did it, but it must have been spectacular because it's the only miracle (other than the resurrection of Jesus himself) that all four gospels tell us about. The people were so impressed that they wanted to make Jesus their king. They didn't understand that he was already a king, but his kingdom was not of this world. He tried to explain that he didn't come to them to feed them free meals, but to feed them with a food that will bring them eternal life. "I am the bread that comes down from heaven, that a person eat it and never die." (Jn. 6,50) Initially as he spoke of himself as the bread of life he was talking about having faith in him and living as he has taught.

Today's gospel, however, continues on with a new theme on Jesus as the bread of life. Not only were they to believe in him, but they were to eat his flesh and drink his blood. If they had some problems with what Jesus had already said, this really blew their minds. Jesus knew this idea really disturbed them, so what did he do? He repeated it with greater emphasis and clarity: "Amen, amen, if you do not eat the flesh of the Son of Man and drink his blood, you have no life in you." (Jn 6,53) And he repeated it again. This is where many in the crowd began to walk away, saying to themselves that Jesus was out of his mind. Jesus didn't call them back to tell them they were misunderstanding him. He knew they understood exactly what he was saying.

This is where many people today part company with Jesus. They don't say he is out of his mind, for they like many of the things he taught. They think his teachings on love and his demonstration of his love for people by forgiving their sins or healing the sick is awesome. They may even call themselves Christians or Catholics, but they find it too much to accept that this consecrated host and sip from the chalice is really Jesus' body and blood. They can't say what Peter did when Jesus asked him if he wanted to leave with the others. Peter said: "Lord, to whom shall we go? It is you who have the words of eternal life; and we have come to believe and are convinced that you are God's Holy One." (Jn 6,68)

We take it on faith when we eat healthy food, take our vitamins, count our calories that this is good for us. We have to take it on faith too that the Eucharist is good for us. "The person who feeds on my flesh and drinks my blood has eternal life (and he remains in me and I in him)." (Jn 6,54&56) We can't go wrong in believing in these words because they come from God himself and God would not lie.

We cannot see with our eyes that bread and wine have been changed into the body and blood of Christ, we can only see that this is so with our mind. We allow our mind to see what our eyes cannot see because we have chosen to believe what Jesus said. As I seek to believe and to visualize the Eucharist as Jesus himself, I find I am helped by modern physics. This is how it works for me: modern physics tells us that a substance may look solid, but it really isn't. That is because everything around us is made of atoms and molecules. There's a lot of space in things, and a lot of energy. If I were to set this podium on fire, what would make it burn? It would burn because of the energy contained in it and the burning would release that energy. If I sit down and eat a sandwich, my body breaks the sandwich down into energy that allows me to keep going. I like to visualize the Eucharist in terms of divine energy. I picture the Holy Spirit transforming the normal energy that's in wheat and wine into divine energy, an energy that somehow creates in us eternal life. What that means, we have yet to find out. We only know that Jesus referred to eternal life as "the fullness of life." (Jn 10,10) No more suffering, pain, growing old, no more wars or hatred and no more death.

Do you want to grow deeper in your faith in the Eucharist. One way I would suggest is to come to Mass one day during the week or to come to a Holy Hour on Wednesday morning or Friday afternoon. I pray that more people will take our Lord's words to heart: "The bread that I shall give is my flesh for the life of the world." (Jn 6,51) Amen.

12th Sunday in Ordinary Time
June 22, 2008

INTRODUCTION – (Jeremiah 20: 10-13, Romans 5: 12-15, Matthew 10: 26-33) The prophet, Jeremiah lived in Israel about 600 years before Christ. The Babylonian destruction of Israel was immanent. The Babylonians came from modern day Iraq. Their capital, Babylon, was located just 100 miles south of Baghdad. Jeremiah was warning God's people that they could avoid the destruction that was on its way if they started living according to God's laws (most of which were being flagrantly ignored or violated. The people didn't like the message, so they decided to kill Jeremiah. His words in today's first reading reflect the pain and misery he experienced for being faithful to his mission. We should not be shocked when we hear him pray that God take vengeance on his persecutors. After all, he was human and not as perfect as Jesus who was able to pray for those who crucified him.

Our first reading leads into the gospel. As we heard last Sunday, Jesus had just chosen his twelve apostles. In today's gospel he prepares to send them out as missionaries. He is warning them their message will not always be well received, they may even suffer and die for it, but they must preach with courage and not be afraid of what might happen to them if they meet rejection.

HOMILY – Pope John Paul II had as his motto: "Be not afraid." Of course, he was quoting our Lord whom we just heard give the same mandate to his apostles in today's gospel, "Do not be afraid." Since God knows how many hairs are on our head and is aware when even a little sparrow dies, then he's aware of every detail of our own lives. Although he is aware, and cares, he does not guarantee us that bad things will not happen to us. Ups and downs are part of our existence and they even happened to God's holy prophets and to Jesus himself. Because God is aware and he cares he tells us not to fear, for he is in control and will make everything turn out right for those who are faithful to him.

"Be not afraid." Sometimes that's easier said than done. Fear is built into us and we feel it when we feel threatened. If fear were not a part of our nature, we wouldn't even exist today, because long ago our ancestors would not have had sense to get out of the way of charging wild animals, saber tooth tigers or poisonous snakes. Nor would we be moved to get out of the way of cars and trucks coming at us 50 miles an hour. Fear enables us to survive, to know when to fight, to know when to run. But sometimes it gets out of control and takes over our life, whether that fear comes from a real threat or an imagined one. Faith is a big help to deal with fear, and sharing our fears with a trusted friend can be helpful, but sometimes fear is so controlling that counseling or medication is required.

I think when Jesus tells us not to fear, he's not talking about the spontaneous reaction we feel when we are threatened, he's telling us not to worry and to put our trust in him that things will come out alright in the end. The words of St. Paul, "We know that all things work for good for those who love God" (Rom 8,28), have been a constant help to me to stay together during very trying times. One thing Jesus does tell us to fear is God! "Do not be afraid of those who can kill the body but cannot kill the soul; rather, be afraid of the one who can destroy both soul and body in Gehenna." In Old Testament times Gehenna was a place of human sacrifice to pagan idols. At the time of Jesus it was a garbage dump, which was constantly burning. Thus Gehenna became the symbol of evil and hell. Jesus' words confuse some people! Aren't we supposed to love God, but if we fear him, how can we love him? Doesn't St. John tell us "perfect love casts out fear?" All of that is true. For those who have a "reward and punishment" view of life, a little fear might help them stay on the straight and narrow. For those who have moved beyond the "reward and punishment" stage, this fear that Jesus talks about is the fear of being unfaithful to God or having a sense of awe, respect and reverence when we approach God. Those who fear God in this way will approach him with awe, respect and reverence frequently. In either case, a little healthy fear of God will greatly reduce our fear of other things in life, including death itself. I know from many years of dealing with people that if we are at peace with God and know the Lord is with us, there will be fewer things in life that can upset us or frighten us. Amen.

13th Sunday in Ordinary Time
June 26, 2005

INTRODUCTION – (2 Kgs 4:8-11, 14-16a, Rom 6:3-4, 8-11, Matt 10:37-42) In our gospel today Jesus tells us we must die to ourselves: "Whoever loses his life for my sake will find it." Today's second reading from Paul tells us that through baptism we have died with Christ and rose with him to share in his divine life. Paul was making reference to the normal way baptism was administered in his day. A person was dunked in the water, symbolizing death and burial and then brought out of the water, symbolizing a resurrection. A person does not have to be baptized by immersion to experience the spiritual effects of the sacrament, namely dying to selfishness and sin and beginning a new life in Christ.

There is a second theme in today's readings: that of kindness to God's holy ones. Jesus is about to send his apostles out as missionaries and he promises them anyone who does a simple act of kindness for them will not lose their reward. In those days there were not hotels and motels. Travelers had to depend on the kindness of others when they traveled. The prophet Elisha in our first reading lived about 800 years before Christ. He often traveled to Mt. Carmel to pray and on his journey to Mt. Carmel he regularly stopped to stay at the home of a couple who lived in a town nearby. The story emphasizes the importance to being receptive to those sent to us by God, whether they be prophets or apostles. The story also shows that if one is kind to one sent by God, God will not let us outdo him in generosity.

HOMILY – We heard Jesus tell us not to let anything or anyone (even those who are closest to us, even our own lives) be more important than he is. He does not make this request for his own glorification. He isn't looking for worldly glory. His life was a life of poverty and simplicity. Besides he has all the glory he needs. He is, after all, Son of God. You can't get any higher than that. He asks us to give him central place in our hearts and in our lives for our own sake and for our own happiness. We'll never really be satisfied in life until we possess and are fully possessed by the life that Christ came to bring us. As St. Augustine said, "Thou hast made us for thyself O Lord and our hearts are restless until they rest in thee."

There are two themes that flow from this basic truth. I think the first message is that the gospel is not always a "feel good" message. Some people only want to hear peace, love and joy when they come to Church. They want a Church that always makes them "feel good." Peace, love and joy are wonderful and Jesus' promises of lasting happiness fill us with hope, and all preachers love to preach about these things, but sometimes, like today, the gospel message is not easy to hear. Being willing to give up everything for Christ, even our own lives (and many people did), is a hard message. Dietrich Bonhoeffer, a Lutheran minister who spent the last two years of his life in prison for resisting Hitler, wrote a lot about "cheap grace," grace that didn't cost us much. Cheap grace means hoping to gain eternal happiness while asking ourselves, "What is the least I can get by with." One of Bonhoeffer's most memorable lines is "When Christ calls a person, he bids him come and die." Following Christ can cost us dearly. If we're afraid of that, if we're always looking for a Church that doesn't really challenge us, then we are not wanting to hear Christ.

The second theme of today's gospel is kindness, especially to those who bring this message of life through death to us. That includes our hierarchy, the priests and religious, but it includes parents and grandparents, neighbors and friends, teachers and spouses and all who have taught us about Christ and who have been models of faith for us. Most of us didn't get our faith out of a textbook. We got it by God's inspiration and by seeing how others lived it. I did come to know some wonderful priests when I was growing up, but most seemed to me to be stuffy and distant. My faith came primarily from my parents and those who taught me in school. And it still is enriched by people I have known and do know now at St. Boniface. When you are here faithfully every week and you pray and sing from your hearts, my spirits are lifted in prayer. So this act of kindness to God's messengers that Jesus promises to reward applies to anyone. A young girl told the story about needing to have her teeth repaired when she was in college. Being a struggling college student, she could hardly afford to have one tooth filled, but the pain was so bad she had to see a dentist. When she went, he wanted to fix all her teeth and she said I can't afford it and started to leave. He understood and said "well, when you finish college you'll get a job and make some money and you can pay me then." He did the job, on credit, and it made a wonderful difference in the way she felt. She was able to pay him off after graduation. She called him a "woodwork angel." She described "woodwork angels" as strangers who come out of nowhere, out of the woodwork, when a person needs help. They may help out with money, skills, protection from danger or from making a big mistake, they may offer us hospitality as the woman did for the prophet Elisha or they may simply offer us a cup of cold water. We all need them. We all need to be one to others. Herman Melville said, "We cannot live only for ourselves. A thousand fibers connect us with our fellow human beings." And Elbert Hubbard said, "People are rich only as they give. He who gives great service gets great returns." Jesus said, "whoever gives only a cup of cold water to one of these little ones to drink because the little one is a disciple – amen, I say to you, he will surely not lose his reward."

14th Sunday in Ordinary Time
July 6, 2008

INTRODUCTION – (Zechariah 9: 9-10, Romans 8: 9, 11-13, Matthew 11: 25-30) Three hundred years is a long time. In our nation, three hundred years would take us back to before George Washington was born and long before our Declaration of Independence. In our first reading we hear from Zechariah the prophet. For those who first heard Zechariah's words, there would have been the realization that it had been three hundred years since their country had a king and had known independence. They could recall their sad history that three hundred years earlier their homes and lands, their city and their Temple had been destroyed and they were exiled to Babylon and became Babylonian slaves. Then the Persians conquered the Babylonians, allowed the Jews to return home, but continued to rule them and to collect taxes from those they ruled. Then came the Greeks who conquered Israel and who eventually bitterly persecuted Jews who would not give up their faith and their traditions. So when the prophet Zechariah tells God's people, "Rejoice!" many of them probably thought he had been out in the sun far too long. But God's prophet has reason to be full of joy. The role of a prophet is to see clearly what others cannot see. He could see a time when there would be no more war, or exile, destruction or conquest. He could see that one day they would have their own king, a king who would bring peace. That is the symbol of the donkey in the first reading. Horses were weapons of war, used by warriors and conquerors. Horses, chariots, warriors' bows and other instruments of war would be outlawed in his kingdom. The people of Jerusalem remembered this prophecy when Jesus came riding into Jerusalem on a donkey on Palm Sunday. We're not at Palm Sunday yet. But we hear in today's gospel Jesus reveals himself as a man of peace who is meek and humble of heart. That's why the passage from Zechariah was chosen for our first reading. Someday after we learn to better follow Jesus, the man of peace, maybe we will then see Zechariah's prophecy of peace fully fulfilled.

HOMILY – Up until a few hundred years ago, the yoke was very common. It would join two animals together so their combined strength could pull a plow or wagon. Now we have trucks and tractors to do the work of animals. The word yoke also had a symbolic meaning. It symbolized slavery and servitude.

At the time of Jesus, the Jewish law sometimes was referred to as a yoke, a burden to be endured. The way the Scribes and Pharisees interpreted God's law certainly proved to be a burden on God's people. (Mt. 23,4) When Jesus said, "take my yoke upon you and learn from me," he was contrasting his way, his teachings to the Jewish leaders' incorrect and burdensome interpretations of God's law that the people would hear weekly in their synagogues. The spirit behind Jesus' teachings would lift their burdens and be refreshing. "Come to me all you who labor and are burdened and I will give you rest." I think there are two ideas that are worth reflecting on. 1) Jesus said "my yoke is easy and my burden light." Every law is a burden, and this includes even the laws Jesus gave us, for law involves obligations and responsibilities, things we have to do and obey. When we obey his law, we discover it is not overburdening, rather it will lift our spirits and will lead us to eternal life. Sin, which is another word for disobedience to God, puts a burden on us. St. Paul tells us when we sin we become indebted to sin. We all know what debt can do to us. It weighs us down. Next week Paul will tell us more about how sin can enslave us, while living according to the Spirit gives us life.

This past week we celebrated our Independence Day. But there's no independence from God. We treasure our freedom in this country, but if we think freedom is doing anything we want, we won't have any freedom at all. I think the image of a sailboat is a good example of what I'm saying. I used to sail a lot. It was important that you kept your hand on the tiller and kept the sail at the right angle to the wind. If you let the boat go free, it would be a disaster. Many times I turned wrong into the wind and got blown over. Once, on a really cold, windy day, I spent a couple of hours in very cold water before someone rescued me. I never told this story before because having to be rescued is embarrassing for a sailor. In our own lives we need to keep going in the right direction to find peace and happiness, and God's laws are meant to keep us going in that direction. God's way is not to limit our freedom as sometimes people think, but to guide us to peace and happiness. When we ignore or violate his law (which is sin) we become a slave to our own worst selves. 2) The other thing about a yoke is that it joins two animals together. With a yoke, one animal does not pull the wagon or the plow alone. When Jesus said, "come to me...take my yoke upon you," he is offering to be our partner in bearing our burdens. He is telling us we won't go through life alone. He promised at the Last Supper he would not leave us orphans (Jn. 14,18) All we need to do, and sometimes we need to do it every day, is to commit ourselves to following him and he will be there for us. We can be sure of that! Amen.

15th Sunday in Ordinary Time
July 13, 2014

INTRODUCTION – (Isaiah 55, 10-11; Romans 8,18-23; Matthew 13,1-9 or 1-23) In today's first reading, the prophet speaks to God's captive people in Babylon (Iraq). After 50 years God began telling them, through the prophet, that their years of captivity and slavery to the Babylonians would soon be ended. They would be able to return to Israel, to their cities, their homes and their farms. Many doubted this could be true. In today's passage God is assuring them his promise will be fulfilled. God compares his word to the rain and the snow. When

God sends moisture to the earth, it does the work of keeping the world green and alive. When God sends out his word, it is not full of empty promises; it is effective and powerful and is able to accomplish what it was sent to do. God's word was true, as roughly 50 years after the exile, the Persians (Iran) destroyed the Babylonian empire and allowed the Jews to return home. In today's gospel parable we are presented with another way of thinking of the power of the word of God: as a seed.

HOMILY – A family were on vacation, and as they rode down the highway there was a big sign that read: Road Closed. They maneuvered around the sign and continued on. Suddenly the road ended and there was an even larger sign: "What part of 'Road Closed?' didn't you understand?" (Reader's Digest, Laughter Really is the Best Medicine, pg 171) In today's gospel Jesus tells us that's why he uses parables, to help those who have trouble understanding his teachings understand what they need to know to be saved.

Today and for the next two Sundays we will hear several of Jesus' parables about the kingdom of heaven. Today's parable and the explanation that goes with it is very clear. God's word is like a seed which can produce life, but if it falls on deaf ears, it produces nothing. It was what Jesus experienced as he traveled from one place to another, teaching. Certainly from the time of Adam and Eve there have been people who hear God's word, and they respond to it like the hardened earth, or stony ground or ground thick with weeds.

A good story, however, can often have several interpretations. So I wish to suggest another way we can look at the parable, a way that might enhance our own spiritual growth. Instead of thinking of the field as all of human kind, think of the entire field as representing just yourself. If I see just myself as the field, I see that sometimes I am closed to God's word, sometimes I get very enthusiastic but my enthusiasm has no depth, sometimes my life is so cluttered with things I have to do or want to do, that I have no time left for God. But sometimes my heart and mind is like the rich soil, and I take God's word in and serve him genuinely and faithfully. Looking at the parable that way, I see in myself hardened paths, stony ground and weeds, but I see also good soil. And I see I have the freedom to determine how well God's word will take root in me by changing what I can in my life so there is more good soil in my heart and mind for the seed of God's word to fall upon.

As we pray today, let us ask God to help us see where in our lives God's grace is having a hard time taking root. Amen.

16th Sunday in Ordinary Time
July 20, 2014

INTRODUCTION – (Wisdom 12: 13,16-19; Romans 8: 26-27; Matthew 13: 24-43) first reading today is from the book of Wisdom, a book of the bible written about 100 years before Christ. At the time, the Jews were being persecuted for their faith by the Greeks. As a consequence, many Jews were giving up their belief in God and converting to the pagan religion and the culture of the Greeks. The author of this book is struggling with the question: "why is God allowing this evil to go on?" His conclusion is that God's way is not to destroy, but to be patient and to lead people to repent. The theme prepares us for the gospel, which also deals with the problem of evil.

HOMILY – Rabbi Harold Kushner writes in his book, When Bad Things Happen to Good People: "Life is not fair. The wrong people get sick and the wrong people get robbed and the wrong people get killed in wars and in accidents." He tells us some people see unfairness and conclude there is no God. Rabbi Kushner argues that the sense of unfairness, the sense of anger and indignation and injustice and sympathy that we feel when these things happen, are in themselves the surest proof of God's reality, for these feelings are planted in our hearts by a God who recognizes unfairness and injustice, who feels anger and indignation and sympathy. But our God is also a patient God who is not ready to come down and destroy his creation for every sin and evil he sees, rather he is ready to come down to call us to holiness and to save us. If God zapped a person every time someone stepped out of line, how many of us would be left? All of what I have been saying is just one attempt among many to understand evil in the world and in our lives. Today's parable of the wheat and the weeds also attempts to find an answer to this mystery.

We don't need to be told there are weeds in God's kingdom. We all know that. The church and its leaders are not always perfect. I like to quote Fr. Andrew Greely who once said "if you ever find a perfect church, by all means join it; just know that once you join it, it will no longer be perfect." Imperfection is all around us, in our nation and other nations, in our friends and members of our family. The important lesson in today's parable is that in the end all things will be made right. The wheat, the good, will shine like the sun in the kingdom of their Father and those who do evil, the weeds, will endure the flames of a fiery furnace. The parable tells us God is the one who is going to make that judgment, but I believe that before we stand before God, we will probably have judged ourselves when we look at how we lived. I believe God will be more merciful on us than we are on ourselves, for as the first reading says in its prayer to God: "Though you are master of might, you judge with clemency, and with much lenience you govern us."

The parable of the wheat and the weeds along with the other two little parables (the mustard seed and the leaven/yeast) are optimistic ones, assuring us that in spite of opposition and persecution the kingdom shall continue growing as well as assuring us of final victory over evil in the end. I think today's parable needs to be heard by our modern culture that tries to tell us that everyone will be saved in the end, no matter whether they were good or evil. The gospel tells us the opposite. Karma is real. The other thing that many people today want to believe is there is no devil. Call it what you will, it is obvious there is a driving force for evil in the world. Personally I believe there is a real devil or devils because I have seen how they operate.

The word for weeds in today's gospel is *Ζιζανία* a specific weed that looks like wheat when it begins to grow, but of course it is only a weed. Sometimes that's the way evil inserts itself into our world, it has the appearance of something good, but it is no good. Just because it looks good doesn't mean it is.

To sum up what I've said: evil will always remain a mystery, and we'll always be struggling against it and struggling to understand it. Don't let its appearance as something good fool you, remember there will be a day of reckoning, there is an invisible force for evil in the world, and God's good kingdom will prevail and overcome all evil in the end. Let's live and pray that we're all on the winning side. Amen.

17th Sunday in Ordinary Time
July 27, 2014

INTRODUCTION – (1 Kings 3,5.7-12; Romans 8,28-30; Matthew 13,44-52) When King David died, his son, Solomon, succeeded him as king of Israel. Today's first reading is Solomon's prayer as he begins his reign. He prayed for an understanding heart that he would reign well. Just think, of all the possible gifts he could have asked for, he chose to ask for wisdom. Observance of God's commands will lead us to wisdom, thus in our reflection on our first reading we praise God in the psalm refrain for his commands and for the wisdom they impart to us.

HOMILY – A woman found a lamp and as she examined it out popped a genie. "Do I get three wishes?" she asked. "Nope, I'm a one-wish genie. What will it be?" She pulled out a map and said "see this map? I want these countries to stop fighting so we can have world peace." "They've been fighting for many centuries. I'm not that good. What else do you have?" the genie asked the lady. "Well, I'd like a good man. One who's considerate, loves kids, is filthy rich, likes to cook, and doesn't watch sports all day." "Okay," the genie said with a sigh. "Let me see that map again." (from Reader's Digest: Laughter Really is the Best Medicine, pg 62)

What would we ask for if God or a one-wish genie appeared to us? When Solomon asked for wisdom it shows he was already wise. Unfortunately he didn't keep using his wisdom to serve God's people well. He married too many wives and spent the country into bankruptcy, so much so that when he died the country split into two kingdoms, pretty much isolating the kings who were descendants of David and Solomon. I felt I needed to add that part about Solomon, because having wisdom does not mean we will always make good use of it. Let us return now to today's gospel. This is the third week now we have been hearing parables about the Kingdom of Heaven. What would we be willing to spend all of our money on, like the people in today's gospel? We may think the parables of the treasure and the pearl need no explanation. Certainly Heaven will be all that we could ever desire and more so. But there is a subtle message here that we must not miss. Notice the persons who discovered the treasure and the pearl made it their highest priority. Nothing else was more important. Our search for the kingdom of God has to be our highest priority. Everything we have attained in life or might attain will give us some satisfaction and happiness, but everything is temporary. Entering into the Kingdom of heaven which Jesus has revealed to us is happiness forever. What could be more important than that?

The parable of the fishing net that gathered up good fish as well as bad is very similar to the parable of the wheat and the weeds. Its message is to trust in God's final judgment and to be patient until that time comes. The perennial problem of evil in the world will be resolved. We have to be careful not to give these parables an interpretation that supports John Calvin's form of predestination. It is true, the wheat and the weeds as well as with the good fish and the bad represent two types of things of superior and inferior quality. John Calvin, the founder of Calvinism would argue God creates people that way too and there's nothing any of us can do to change it. In Calvin's view God creates us destined to either heaven or hell, and we cannot change our destiny. To think that way would contradict the entire message of the gospel. We are called to holiness and we have a free will to choose God's grace or to disregard it. Remember it is in Matthew's gospel that we read the account of the Last Judgment where the "Son of Man" will separate peoples of all nations inviting one group to enter the kingdom of Heaven and commanding the other to depart from him into the everlasting fire. It is on this basis that they are separated: on the basis of "what you have done for the least of my brothers and sisters you did it for me." Weeds can't change their nature, nor can fish that are inedible, but because we are human with a free will, we can change ourselves, with God's help, when our life is going in the wrong direction.

The correct way to think of "predestination" is that we are all predestined to heaven, a place "prepared for us from the beginning of the world" as Jesus calls it (Mt. 25,34), but the gospels tell us not everyone lives up to the destiny God has created them for.

There is a strange image at the end of the parable about the fish, that the bad fish will be thrown into a furnace of fire. Usually bad fish are just thrown back into the water. This image of being thrown into a furnace of fire and the weeping and gnashing of teeth is symbolic language for eternal suffering.

Jesus asked his disciples "Have you understood all these things?' Let us pray for the wisdom to understand, not as with the wisdom of Solomon but with the wisdom of a faithful disciple of Jesus. Amen.

18th Sunday in Ordinary Time
July 31, 2011

INTRODUCTION – (Isaiah 55:1-3; Roman 8:35, 37-39; Matthew 14:13-21) Today's first reading is an invitation to the Jews who had been exiled in Babylon for 50 years. Surely by this time very few Jews were still living who had ever seen Jerusalem. Yet those in exile had heard stories about the land they lost and were yearning to return home. The prophet we hear this morning tells them they are free to do so. His message covers 15 chapters in the latter part of the Book of Isaiah. Their liberation was happening through the benevolence of the Persian King, Cyrus, who had been able to conquer the Babylonians. Through King Cyrus, God was fulfilling his promise that he would bring his people back to their own land, a land flowing with milk and honey. They would now find nourishment from their own lands. If the food God provided for them sounds pretty basic: grain, bread, wine, milk, it must have sounded like a lavish banquet to an oppressed people. Our first reading prepares us for the gospel which is also about food.

HOMILY – If you think it's hot here, imagine what it must be like in Texas. Rumor has it that the mosquitoes are flying around with canteens. The farmers are giving crushed ice to their chickens to keep them from laying hard-boiled eggs. A fire hydrant was seen bribing a dog. The Baptists are starting to baptize by sprinkling, the Methodists are using wet-wipes, the Presbyterians are giving out rain-checks and the Catholics are praying for the wine to change back into water.

For the past three weeks, we have heard seven parables about the kingdom of heaven. Jesus didn't just preach about the kingdom, he demonstrated it. He demonstrated it in casting out demons, healing the sick, raising the dead, forgiving sins and in feeding the multitude.

Last week I dedicated a significant portion of my homily to the apocalyptic vision that was current around the time of Jesus. The general notion of apocalypticism was that the world was suffering under the dominion of evil forces. But God would soon overthrow the forces of evil (including, and especially, the enemies of Israel) and establish his good kingdom. Those who lived good lives would enjoy the blessings of the kingdom while those who were evil would be excluded from the kingdom. Moreover, apocalyptic expectations at the time of Jesus were that this new world over which God would reign would come about in a very short time. Knowing something about apocalyptic thinking is a great help in understanding the gospel for preparing ourselves for God's good kingdom is the basic message of Jesus. We heard the prophet in today's first reading telling God's people, in poetic terms, that God alone can give them what they need. The prophet uses the image of grain and bread, water, wine and milk and rich fare all for free – all they have to do is to come to God and not go away from him as they had done. Going away from God is what led to the exile in the first place. Jesus used a similar image a couple of times when he told about the kingdom: the parable that is probably most familiar is the one that tells us the kingdom is like a king who gave a wedding feast for his son, when many of those invited excused themselves from what would have been a grand event. (The recent royal wedding of William and Kate would perhaps have been comparable to the wedding in Jesus' parable, except that in Jesus' culture, wedding celebrations would go on for a few days). (Matthew 22:2).

So when Jesus fed a great crowd in a miraculous way, it would not be surprising if the people saw this as a sign of God's kingdom and Jesus as the king who would initiate it. St. John tells us as much: "When the people saw the sign he had done, they said, 'This is truly the Prophet, the one who is to come into the world.'" John adds: "Since Jesus knew that they were going to come and carry him off to make him king, he withdrew again to the mountain alone." (John 6:14-15)

There is no doubt that the early Church retold this story of the multiplication of the loaves using Eucharistic language. They saw the Eucharist as God continuing to feed his people with rich food and choice wine – Jesus' own body and blood. Thus the story of the feeding in this deserted place (tradition has it on the shore of the Sea of Galilee) has actions similar to what Jesus did at the Last Supper: he took, he blessed, he broke and he gave the loaves at the miraculous feeding and the bread at the Last Supper.

John the Baptist was Jesus' cousin and most likely his friend. We have hints that Jesus began his ministry as a follower of John the Baptist. The gospel today tells us that when John was put to death, Jesus withdrew by himself. Most likely he needed some time to grieve. But the disciples and the crowd caught up with him. He put his own personal needs aside when he saw the crowd. Matthew and Luke tell us he cured the sick; Mark tells us he taught them. (He probably did both.) As the day began to fade, the issue of food came up. The gospel does not tell us in detail how Jesus achieved this marvelous event, only through faith can we believe that Jesus fed 5000 men (not counting women and children) with five loaves and two fish. The Lord continues to feed us in a miraculous way today – a mysterious feeding that also requires our faith. In the Eucharist today we also have a sign of the coming kingdom, when we will be united with Jesus our Lord and savior forever. Paul confirms this when he tells us in the second reading that, in spite of our unworthiness, nothing in all of creation will separate us from his love. Amen.

Transfiguration
August 6, 2006

INTRODUCTION – Our first reading is from the book of Daniel (Dn. 7:7-10, 13- 14). The author of this book lived during the time the Greeks dominated most of the known world. The Greeks were trying to get everyone to follow their religion (paganism) and any Jew who remained faithful to his or her Jewish faith was put to death. This was the first time in the history of the world that people were persecuted for their beliefs. The book of Daniel tried to offer the Jewish people hope: hope of a savior. This salvation comes from one like a "son of man" whom God endows with kingship and power. Our reading is one of Daniel's visions and it first describes God who is called the Ancient One - indicating God's eternity. The term "son of man" means simply a human being, but this "son of man" would be unique and would be the savior of God's people. This was the favorite title Jesus used in referring to himself. The glory of God is described in today's first reading. It is shown through Christ in his Transfiguration, which is described in today's gospel (Mk. 9:2-10), and in today's second reading from the Second Letter of St. Peter (1:16-19).

HOMILY – Last Sunday I said that for the next four weeks we would be hearing from the sixth chapter of St. John on the Eucharist. I hadn't looked ahead to see that this Sunday fell on August 6th which is the feast of the Transfiguration. Although we hear about the Transfiguration every year on the second Sunday of Lent, the actual feast of the Transfiguration is on August 6. It is an important enough feast that it replaces the normal Sunday liturgy.

Tradition identifies Mt. Tabor as the mountain of the Transfiguration. It's quite a climb to get to the top. There is a chapel on top of the mountain commemorating the occasion of the Transfiguration. I said Mass there sixteen years ago when I went with a study group to the Holy Land. They had cars and buses to take us up the mountain. I'm not surprised that Peter, James and John fell asleep, as St. Luke tells us in his gospel, when they went there with Jesus. They didn't have cars and buses and they would have been very tired when they got to the top. But when they woke up their efforts to make it up to the top of that mountain with Jesus were well rewarded. "It is good that we are here," Peter said. "Let us make three tents here: one for you, one for Moses and one for Elijah." It sounds to me as if they were ready to stay there for several weeks, it was such an awesome experience. As wonderful as it was, Jesus' work wasn't finished and neither was theirs. They had to come back down to earth.

Most of us, I'm sure, have had moments when we've felt God's presence and closeness and special love, or when we knew God was helping us with some problem.

But I'm sure there are few, if any of us, who have experienced anything like the Transfiguration. We may be a mystic and have ecstatic experiences in prayer or we may be a saint who receives visions of Jesus or Mary. Other than that, we've probably not experienced anything like the Transfiguration and may find it difficult to relate to. But we can learn from it.

(1) We can learn that God has great glory reserved for us until, as the second reading tells us, "day dawns and the morning star rises in your hearts."

(2) We can learn from what God spoke on the holy mountain about Jesus: "this is my beloved Son, listen to him." This is not something new, of course, but it doesn't hurt to be reminded once again that we must listen to him.

(3) We can learn that we cannot expect mountain-top experiences every day when we pray, when we receive the sacraments, when we keep the Commandments. There are those moments when we get a lot of consolation and good feelings from our faith and our prayers. Then there are those moments when prayer is dry, when our faith is exactly what that word means, believing only on the word of another and not feeling anything except that we're in a desert. The apostles were with Jesus three years and there was only one experience like the Transfiguration, and only three of them experienced it. Our religion can't be based on feelings. It's based on faith in God and love for God and for one another. Sometimes we feel it and sometimes we don't. It's not how we feel it that counts, but how we live it.

(4) Another thing we can learn from the Transfiguration is that we can't always trust appearances. In appearance Jesus looked pretty much like the rest of us. Artists have pictured him with a halo, but I'm sure there was no halo when people saw him every day. The gospels would have remarked about it if there were. For a brief moment on Mt. Tabor, the apostles saw and heard things that indicated there was a lot more to Jesus than they ever imagined.

Today, as we come to Mass, our faith calls us to look beyond appearances. When we receive Communion, we receive what appears to be a wafer of bread and a sip of wine, but faith in the power and the words of Jesus tells us this host and cup offers us so much more. It is food for eternal life. We pray as always that the Lord will help us to know his presence with us today, and if we do not experience that presence, we pray for the faith to be able to see beyond appearances and still be able to say as Peter did on the mountain: "it is good that we are here."

19th Sunday in Ordinary Time
August 7, 2011

INTRODUCTION – (1 Kings 19:9a, 11-13a; Romans 9:1-5; Matthew 14:22-33) Our first reading today takes us back roughly 860 years before Christ. It was the time of Elijah the prophet. Ahaz was king in Israel, but the real power behind the throne was the infamous Queen Jezebel. Jezebel was an impassioned promoter of paganism of the worship of the Canaanite god Baal. Elijah, of course, was just as passionate in trying to keep God's people faithful to the God of Israel. So you might imagine they would clash and they did. Elijah challenged all the prophets of Baal to a contest on Mt. Carmel which ended in Elijah's victory and the annihilation of all the pagan prophets. Certainly Christ would not have handled it the way Elijah did, but Christ wouldn't be born for another eight and a half centuries. In spite of the obvious outcome of the contest, which proved Israel's God was the true God, Jezebel was furious and vowed blood vengeance on Elijah. To save his life, Elijah fled from Israel to Mt. Horeb in Sinai, the very same place where Moses gave Israel the Ten Commandments and where God made a covenant with Israel. There Elijah heard God's voice, not in dramatic natural phenomena, but in the silence of his heart.

HOMILY – A doctor phoned his patient one afternoon and told him: "I have some bad news and some worse news. The bad news is that all your tests show you have 24 hours to live." The patient said, "What could be worse than that?" The doc answered, "I've been trying to reach you since yesterday."

Pope John Paul II became pope in October, 1978. There was lots of bad news then. The cold war was threatening world peace. Modern culture was destroying traditional social and moral values. Priests and nuns were abandoning their vocations in huge numbers. Conservatives and liberals were battling over the implementation of Vatican II. His message to the Church and the world at the beginning of his long pontificate are the words we hear in today's gospel: "Be not afraid."

Fear, of course, is a healthy thing when it motivates us to protect ourselves from some threat to the wellbeing of ourselves or of those we love. Fear stimulates us emotionally to prepare for fight or flight. But a lot of people are consumed by fears that are groundless, irrational, or certain things we can do nothing about except pray.

In last week's gospel, we heard about Jesus miraculously feeding over 5000 people with five loaves of bread and two fish. Matthew immediately follows that gospel with today's gospel. The miraculous feeding took place on the sea of Galilee. Jesus made the disciples get into a boat and he went off to the hills alone to pray. Matthew leaves us to wonder why Jesus acted this way. St. John fills in some of the details. John tells us that after the crowd had seen what Jesus did in healing the sick and feeding all of them, they decided they were going to make him their king. As king, he would be their liberator and savior. He would raise an army and drive the Romans out of Israel and Judea. He would rule them, maybe even fulfill every need they had. Jesus knew that's not what the Father sent him to do. As savior he had much greater things to offer them than freedom from the powers of Rome and free meals. So Jesus sent the Apostles away because he knew they would be particularly excited over the prospect of Jesus taking over as king. Some of them already imagined themselves having important places in Jesus' kingdom. So he sent them off, away from the crowd, dismissed the crowd himself and went off alone to pray.

The story of Jesus walking on the water is an unusual miracle. Usually when Jesus worked a miracle, he was responding to someone's needs: hunger, sickness, evil spirit possession, storms on the sea. Jesus walking on the water is simply a manifestation of his divine nature. There are numerous references in the Old Testament to God walking on the water or the sea. Seeing him approaching them, the Apostles panicked and Jesus said: "take courage, it is I, be not afraid." "It is I" is an important part of this gospel because it gives greater clarity about what this event meant. It could mean, "it's just me." But it is also in Greek the name that God gave Moses when Moses wanted to know God's name: "I am," or "I am who I am." "ἐγώ εἰμί" All Jews knew this sacred name but no one ever pronounced it except the High Priest once a year in the Holy of Holies. Why does Jesus wish to reveal himself in this way? First of all it is important to note that in all three gospels that tell the story of Jesus walking on water, it immediately follows the story of the miraculous feeding and is linked to it. If you remember last week, the miraculous feeding anticipated the Eucharist in that it tells us Jesus took bread, blessed it, broke it and gave it. These are the same verbs used at the Last Supper in the account of the institution of the Eucharist. The Eucharistic symbolism that begins with the miracle of the feeding continues into the story of walking on the water. There we have the Apostles struggling in the night, with the wind against them, feeling as if they were making no progress. Suddenly Jesus assures them of his presence. He would not desert them. You might recall his words at the Last Supper: "I will not leave you orphans". He brings courage and calms their fears by announcing his presence, which he will also do for us, and which he especially does in the Eucharist when he tells us: "this is my body," "this is my blood."

Matthew joins a story about Peter to his account of Jesus walking on the water. It points out the special position of Peter as do many other passages in the New Testament. It also shows Peter that, with Christ's bidding and with his help, Peter would be able to do amazing things. So can any of us when our Lord invites us to follow him and is there to hold us up. I can't say how many times the presence, especially in the Eucharist, strengthened me and helped me in difficult times. So he is with us now at Mass today telling us as he told the Apostles: "be not afraid." Amen.

Vigil & Feast of the Assumption
August 15, 2000

INTRODUCTION AT THE VIGIL – (1 Chr 15:3-4, 15-16; 16:1-2; 1 Cor 15:5b- 57; Luke 11:27-28) It is a dogma of our faith that at the end of her life, Mary, like her son, was taken body and soul into heaven. This is the meaning of the Assumption, whose vigil we celebrate this evening.

Our first reading is about the Ark of the Covenant, the sacred gold plated box that contained the Ten Commandments and on top of which were two golden angels (similar to the two angels on our tabernacle doors if you can see them.) The Ark was the unique symbol of God's presence with Israel. It was constructed in the desert after Moses and the Israelites left Egypt. It led them into the Promised Land. Often it was taken into battle with them. When King David established his capital in Jerusalem about the year 1000 BC, he brought the Ark there. Today's reading describes this solemn and joyful occasion. After the temple was built, the Ark was placed in the Holy of Holies and there it remained for 400 years until the Babylonians destroyed the temple. In Christian symbolism, Mary is sometimes referred to as the Ark of the Covenant. As the Ark represented the special presence of God dwelling with his people, Mary carried within herself Jesus who is truly Son of God dwelling with us.

MASS DURING THE DAY: (Rev 11:19a; 12:1-6a, 10ab; 1 Cor 15:20-27; Luke 1: 39-56) It is a dogma of our faith that at the end of her life, Mary, like her son, was taken body and soul into heaven. This is the meaning of the Assumption, the feast we celebrate today. In our first reading from Revelation, we hear about a woman, a child and a dragon. The dragon is the devil and the powers of evil at work in the world. The child is Christ. The woman in our reading has a double symbolism. She stands for Mary, the physical mother of Jesus Christ and she stands for the Church, our spiritual mother who brings Jesus Christ to birth in us through faith and the sacraments. The glorious way in which the woman is described has a double symbolism too. It symbolizes the glory of Mary in the assumption and it also symbolizes the glory which we, the faithful, the Church, hope to enjoy one day.

HOMILY – St. Francis de Sales asks the simple question in his sermon for the Assumption: "What son would not bring his mother back to life and would not bring her into paradise after her death if he could?" Who could argue with a statement like that? In Mary's Assumption the glory of Jesus' resurrection is first of all extended to his mother, but as we celebrate it we celebrate likewise our own hope to share in this risen glory some day. We recite this belief in the last lines of the creed: "We believe in the resurrection of the dead, and the life of the world to come."

It's interesting that the Holy Father declared the dogma of the Assumption during a difficult time in recent history. In 1950, when the doctrine of the Assumption was declared by Pope Pius XII, we had experienced two world wars, the Holocaust, the Atomic Bomb and the beginning of the Cold War. The world had enough reason to feel hopeless. Contrasted with the pessimism of the time, this dogma offers hope, hope that the destiny of the human race is more than wars, destruction and devastation. At about that same time in 1950, the cult of the body and the glories of sexuality were beginning to take hold of society. The Church leaders could see that the more that sex and the body were idolized the more society would lose its respect for marriage and family values. In contrast to the glorification of the body as an object of pleasure, this dogma affirms the true dignity and the beauty of the body and the source of that dignity and beauty which is God's grace within us.

In the Assumption Mary is fully united with her son in glory. She remains his mother. He remains her son. Cardinal Suenens once said, "Jesus does not point out Mary and say, 'She used to be my mother.'" Not only is she Jesus' mother, she is our mother too, for on Calvary Jesus gave her to us to be our mother. "Woman, behold your son," he said to her and to St. John, who was a representative of all disciples, Jesus said "Behold your mother." We know and believe that Mary is concerned about our salvation. We expect Mary to help us and we pray to her. Protestants sometimes have trouble with this idea of praying to Mary. Jesus is our savior and we all believe that. But Protestants believe we should pray for one another. If we can ask others to pray for us and we pray for them, why can't those in heaven also pray for us? Are we now so separated from those who have died so that they no longer can help us or be concerned about us? If we seek the prayers of sinners on earth, for we are all sinners, why not seek the intercession of the saints in heaven? Why not turn to the Queen of saints, God's own Mother?

The Assumption tells us that God is not only concerned about our souls but also about our bodies. They are temples of the Spirit. They are part of who we are, and so the feast of the Assumption is a feast that celebrates who we shall be. In addition to the Arc of the Covenant being a symbol for Mary, there is an another way in which today's first reading connects with today's feast. In Christian literature, especially in the book of Revelation, Jerusalem symbolizes our heavenly home. Thus, the Ark being taken to Jerusalem symbolized Mary being taken body and soul into the heavenly kingdom.

20th Sunday in Ordinary Time
August 14, 2011

INTRODUCTION – (Isaiah 56:1, 6-7; Romans 11:13-15, 29-32; Matthew 15:21- 28) Our theme is expressed in the psalm refrain: "O God, let all the nations praise you." God wants all nations and all people to know him and love him, and God desires to share his love with all people. We take this for granted. However, the first believers in Christ were Jewish. They insisted that for Gentiles to become believers, they first had to become Jews and be circumcised and follow all the Jewish rituals and customs, fasting obligations, restricted diet and temple sacrifices. We read in the Acts of the Apostles that Peter at first, and then Paul, said, "no way would all that be required – salvation comes through Christ who is the fulfillment of the Law." The Apostles and early Christians insisted that the moral obligations of the law needed to be observed (such as the Ten Commandments), but the fight was over as to whether Gentile Christians had to observe Jewish cultic and ritual laws. Our first reading, a passage from the Book of Isaiah (written 500 years before Christ), foretells that Gentiles (called "foreigners" in the reading) would someday worship in God's Temple and could even offer sacrifices. Even 500 years later, during Jesus' time, Jews were very exclusive as to their special claim on God. For example, there were major divisions as to where people could go when they came to the Temple. The courtyard of the priests was closest to the Temple itself, next closest was the courtyard for Jewish men, then further out was the courtyard for Jewish women, then furthest from the Temple itself was the courtyard of the Gentiles. Gentiles were forbidden by death to go beyond their section. Isaiah, in today's first reading, is proposing an extremely radical concept that Gentiles would offer sacrifice in the Temple. There is even a hint further on in Isaiah that some of the Gentiles would be chosen to be priests and Levites. How this ties in with the gospel I will explain at the end of my homily.

HOMILY – This is a poem that always made me smile. It's entitled Semantics:

Call a woman a kitten, but never a cat; You can call her a mouse, cannot call her a rat; Call a woman a chicken, but never a hen; Or you surely will not be her caller again. You can call her a duck, cannot call her a goose; You can call her a deer, but never a moose; You can call her a lamb, but never a sheep; Economic she lives, but you can't call her cheap. You can say she's a vision, can't say she's a sight; And no woman's skinny, she's slender and slight. If she should burn you up, say she sets you afire, And you'll always be welcome, you tricky old liar.

This poem illustrates how two different words, close in meaning, can evoke very different reactions. In today's gospel, Jesus meets a pagan woman, a Greek, living in the neighborhood of Tyre and Sidon. The area itself tells us she was probably a financially well-to-do person. She was a woman who was a loving mother and a very clever person. This is a unique story. I cannot think of any other story where Jesus seems so harsh with someone seeking his help. It's also the only one I can think of where someone got the better of Jesus in a debate. I would guess that the only part of this story that most people remember is Jesus saying to her "it is not right to take the food of the children (the Jews) and throw it to the dogs (meaning Gentiles)." referring to someone as a dog in those days, as well as today, would be an insult. A dog would be an unclean animal for the Jews, just as Gentiles were considered unclean by the Jews. What if Jesus had said: "it is not right to take the food of the children and throw it to the birds?" Birds were unclean, too, for Jews. Would that have been less offensive? Actually in the Greek, the word that is used here generally means a puppy or a pet, rather than a mangy cur that just freely roamed the neighborhood. Was puppy offensive? I guess we'll never know which word would be most cutting. The important thing to notice is that the woman didn't turn and walk away in a huff. She was humble enough and clever enough and persistent enough to accept Jesus' remark and turn it to her advantage in order to gain his help to heal her daughter.

I have brief comments before I conclude. In the gospel, the healing is not the primary focus of the story. It is the conversation between Jesus and the woman. In that we find a lesson for ourselves. How many times have we prayed earnestly for something, something very dear to us, and God seems to have ignored us or rebuffed us. We turn on our heels and walk away, angry, promising we will quit praying or going to Church or thinking God just doesn't care about me. Jesus has on other occasions in the gospels insisted on the importance of perseverance in prayer and not giving up. The woman in the gospel wouldn't give up.

A second point goes back to what I said in my introduction, to the issue the early Church was dealing with about the conversion of the Gentiles (do they have to become Jews before they could become Christians). Fortunately the issue was settled long ago and we don't have to deal with it. But surely this story of the Canaanite woman would have been on the minds of those who lived during the first century after Jesus. It's most likely this is precisely why the evangelists recorded the event. The story shows that although Jesus' mission was not to the Gentiles before he was crucified, he was not opposed to their having a full share in God's love and blessings. If the early Church had decided Gentiles must first become Jews in order to share in God's kingdom, the gospel probably would not have spread as widely and as rapidly as it did. Thus, we might never have come to know about Jesus except as some obscure person in history. And so, every Sunday, as we do today, we come together to hear about Jesus and to celebrate the love God has for us and for all people. Amen.

21st Sunday in Ordinary Time
August 24, 2008

INTRODUCTION – (Isaiah 22:19-23, Romans 11: 33-36, Matthew 16:13-20) Shebna was a powerful man in the court of King Hezekiah in Judah, 700 years before Christ. Next to the king, he had the most powerful position in the kingdom. Shebna's power went to his head and he used his position to exploit the poor and the innocent in order to make himself exorbitantly rich. God said through Isaiah that Shebna needed to be replaced by a person with integrity. The only reason this passage was selected for today's reading was because of the reference to the key of the House of David. Keys are symbols of authority. In our gospel Jesus promises he would give Peter the keys to the kingdom of heaven.

HOMILY – I want to make a point about something I saw in the Enquirer this past week, then I want to reflect on two important ideas in today's gospel. There was a brief news clip in Thursday's paper about a hacker who broke into the telephone system of FEMA last weekend and racked up about $12,000 in long distance phone calls to the Middle East and Asia. FEMA is part of Homeland Security. I didn't feel real secure after reading that! If this isn't a good incentive for people to pray for our country and our world, I don't know what is. Psalm 127 says: "If the Lord does not build the house, in vain do its builders labor; if the Lord does not watch over the city, in vain does the watchman keep vigil." We live in a society that keeps us so busy that often prayer is relegated to "something I'll do when I have the time."

We are constantly being told our government is doing a great job of protecting us and I can only assume they are doing the best they can, but can we depend totally on the government? When was the last time we actually asked God to help our country. You might say a hacker breaking into a department of Homeland Security phone system and charging $12,000 in long distance phone calls is just a small thing, and maybe it is, but wars have been won and lost over seemingly small things. I say all this, not with the intent of frightening people, but with the intent of reminding all of us we need to constantly pray. "If the Lord does not watch over the city, in vain does the watchman keep vigil."

Now I want to reflect on two important ideas in today's gospel. First of all there are many places in the Scriptures that emphasize the preeminent position of Peter among the apostles, but there are two places where Peter's position of leadership is spelled out more clearly than anywhere else. The one is in St. John where Jesus tells Peter after the resurrection: "Feed my lambs, feed my sheep." Also in Scripture where Peter's position of importance is clearly emphasized is in today's gospel. Such insistence on the position of Peter vis-à-vis the other apostles is what underlies our belief that after Christ, the Holy Father is chief shepherd and head of the Church. His role is to be the visible representative of Christ. This doesn't mean he has perfectly represented Christ at all times in history, but that is still the position he holds. He has the final word on any issue relating to the Church. The keys Jesus said he would give Peter symbolize this authority. The keys Jesus gave Peter were not buried with him and that position of authority did not end when Peter died. It was passed on to his successors. This is implied in the gospel Matthew wrote, for Peter had been dead for at least 25 or 30 years when Matthew wrote this passage. Matthew made a big issue of this incident, not to tell us about some personal favor Jesus bestowed on Peter, but because the leadership position of Peter would remain as part of the structure of

Christ's community of believers.

A second important idea in today's gospel is the answer to the question Jesus asked his apostles: "Who do you say that I am?" How we answer this question will determine how each of us relates to him. Is he, for example, someone worth our time on Sunday or even during the week? Is he someone we can trust? Is he someone who loves us, forgives us, wants only the best for us? Is he someone who has the authority to tell us how to live, what we should do, what we may not do? Is he someone we look forward to spending eternity with? Can any of us give a complete and perfect answer to that question "Who do you say that I am?" In one way or another, each week I try to help you have a better sense of how to answer this question, even as I try to answer it for myself. It's easy to say Jesus is savior, Jesus is messiah, Jesus is Son of God, or as we say in the creed each week: Jesus is "God from God, light from light, true God from true God, etc." But has our mind and heart connected with these words to the extent that we can exclaim with Paul: "Oh, the depth of the riches and wisdom and knowledge of God! ... For from him and through him and for him are all things." The apostles could tell Jesus what others said about him, and we can also say what others have said about Jesus. That's okay, for that's how we begin to learn who Jesus is, by what others tell us. But have we moved beyond what others have told us to know Jesus in a personal way, a way that Jesus could say has not been revealed to us by "flesh and blood, but by the Heavenly Father?" If we do not know Jesus personally, what can we do that will help us to know him, not just by hearsay, but in a deeply personal way? How we do it is how we get to know anyone in a personal way. By spending time with a person. There are no shortcuts. Spending time with God, with Jesus, is called prayer.

That's what we are about now. Amen.

22nd Sunday in Ordinary Time
August 28, 2005

INTRODUCTION – (Jeremiah 20, 7–9) Our first reading goes back about 600 B.C. The author of our passage is the prophet Jeremiah. Apparently he thought that people would be grateful to him for speaking God's word to them. But his job of telling them to change their ways and get right with God only made them hate him. The people ridiculed him, threw him in jail and even tried to kill him. We hear him complaining to God "You duped me! You tricked me, God!" I'm sure it wasn't the first time God heard the complaint that life is not fair. Jesus' faithfulness to his mission would bring him suffering too, but Jesus was well aware of what was going to happen to him as we hear him warn his disciples in today's gospel. In last Sunday's gospel Jesus praised Peter for acknowledging Jesus as the Messiah. Jesus even promised Peter the keys to the kingdom of heaven. But Peter wasn't ready for all this talk about suffering and when Peter tried to talk Jesus out of the idea Jesus called him Satan. That's because Peter was trying to tempt Jesus away from being faithful to his calling.

HOMILY – (Matthew 16, 21–27) Jesus tells us "whoever wishes to come after me must deny himself, take up his cross, and follow me." At the time St. Matthew was writing, this was literally true for many Christians. It still happens in some parts of the world that those who believe in Christ and follow him end up paying for it with their lives. Do not misunderstand Jesus' statement. When Jesus said "whoever wishes to come after me must take up his cross and follow me," that does not mean that if we decide not to follow him we're not going to have any problems or crosses. If we choose not to follow him in order to avoid the difficulties that might be demanded of us, problems will find us anyway. Problems and crosses are part of everyone's life, whether they believe in Christ or not. And since Christ came to show us the way to peace and joy, avoiding the hardships involved with following him will only cost us more dearly in the long run. Religion and philosophy have always tried to understand the mystery of suffering, especially the difficult problem of why good people suffer. So many different explanations are out there. None of them can take all the mystery out of suffering. For me, the best answer is found in the gospel. Jesus through his cross and resurrection has given us hope in our pain and hopelessness and has shown us suffering can lead to glory, if we will accept our crosses along with him. That requires total faith in him.

Now Peter, whom we heard in today's gospel, had faith in Jesus. If you recall last week's gospel he said of Jesus: "you are the Christ, the Son of the living God." That profession of faith was made just minutes before the scene in today's gospel. When Jesus began talking about suffering Peter objected. Peter professed that he believed in Jesus as the Messiah, the Christ, but Peter didn't think the Messiah should have to suffer. Peter had Jesus' career path all figured out. Peter's faith in Jesus was way too limited. He couldn't see what Jesus was seeing and was trying to tell them. He couldn't see that if Jesus was determined to be faithful to his mission of teaching and healing, which he was, being faithful would cost him his life. Jesus scolded Peter and called him Satan because he was trying to tempt Jesus away from faithfully staying with his calling. Jesus told him: "you are thinking not as God does, but as human beings do."

That sounds almost unfair of Jesus to say: "You're thinking not as God does!" How are we expected to think like God thinks? If we tried really hard, do you suppose we could? With only our human brains to think with, we can only think like human beings do. But there is something that helps us think like God does. It's faith! Faith enables us to go beyond our own limited human capabilities. It's just like learning from any great teacher, when God tells us something and we truly believe it, we're seeing things and knowing things God sees and knows, even if we can't fully grasp everything at once. We're beginning to think like God does. Now I interrupt this homily for a brief commercial.

If we are grateful to have the faith and hope in Christ that we have, isn't this something we would like to share? One way we do this is though our RCIA program which begins this Wednesday evening. Everyone who has gone through our RCIA reports having enjoyed it. If you know anyone who might be interested in knowing more about Christ and the Church, please invite them or better yet, come with them. In a similar vein, we still have room in our school for some more students. All our children receive an excellent education as well as an education about Jesus Christ and his teachings, whether they are Catholic or not. We have a great principal and a great staff. And if a family needs help with tuition there is a very good possibility of getting it. End of commercial.

Coming to Mass, as we are doing now, teaches us to think as God does. We listen to what he tells us in the Scriptures. And we celebrate in a mysterious way Jesus' death and resurrection. In that event we are given a vision of God's plan for all who live in his grace. Amen.

23rd Sunday in Ordinary Time
September 7, 2014

INTRODUCTION – (Ezekiel 33,7-9; Romans 13, 8-10; Matthew 18, 15-20) Our first reading takes us back six hundred years before Christ as God explains to his prophet Ezekiel his responsibility as a prophet. Ezekiel must warn God's people of their sinful ways or Ezekiel himself will be held accountable. It is a prelude to the gospel where Jesus instructs his followers how to help each other stay on the right track. St. Paul's teaching on love in our second reading reminds us that if we should try to correct one another, it should be done out of love.

HOMILY – I want to tell you a little story. A lady I know, I will call her Agnes, is a loving mother and grandmother. She has a friend who has been alienated from some of her family for a long time. Since Agnes' own family is very close to each other, Agnes made a decision, hoping that alienation or separation would never be part of her own family. In addition to praying for her family, which she always did, she approached one of her adult grandchildren who was highly respected by the other family members. Agnes asked him to be the mediator for any problems that might arise in the future. If ever there was a chance people would become alienated from one another, or there would be fighting or hatred among family members, he would step in. Agnes went so far as to instruct him in what to say. "Tell them I put you in charge of keeping the family together and to straighten things out. You are in charge." It was a heavy responsibility for him to accept, but because he loved his grandmother, he promised to do as she asked. Grandmother, who is dearly loved and respected by her family, is also very wise. It gave her peace, knowing that when she had passed on, someone will be watching out for the family and helping to keep them together. She took the burden off her grandson, so that if he does try to deal with some sensitive family issues, he won't be rejected for sticking his nose in someone else's business. He can say "Grandma left me in charge of helping to keep our family united."

Jesus is very wise too. He is telling his followers that same thing in today's gospel: "I want you to be in charge of straightening things out when there are problems and disagreements and fights and when people make up their own rules that lead my followers into separation and disunity." We, you and I and the rest of the Church, who have been put in charge have done a far from perfect job in this regard with so much division among Christ's followers. In theological language we refer to this as "fraternal correction;" that is, correcting a brother or sister who is being led astray from the many teachings of Christ, especially the one very dear to his heart, "that all may be one." Obviously, Jesus is talking about some major problems here when he outlines these three steps that, hopefully, may lead a straying or offending member of the community back toward reconciliation.

Jesus taught us, though, that before we go correcting other people, we should look to ourselves first. There is a story about a mother in India whose son had an insatiable desire for sweets, and she brought him a long way to talk to Gandhi, so he would convince her son not to eat so many sweets. Gandhi told her to bring her son back in two weeks. When mother and son returned two weeks later, Gandhi told the boy to stop eating so much sugar and the boy agreed. The mother asked Gandhi: "why did you not just say this to the boy two weeks ago and save me the hardship of traveling back here?" Gandhi replied "Two weeks ago I ate too many sweets. I needed to see if I could stop before I counseled the boy." (Celebration: Sept 7, 2014 - Homily) Jesus tells us if we try to take the gnat out of our brother or sister's eye, we first need to remove the beam from our own eye. (Mt. 7,3)

It is a delicate thing to remind someone that what they are doing is not right. In my ministry, I have had successful and rewarding moments when I have seen people respond to my encouragement to make some change in how they were living, on the other hand I have also been told to "get lost." Even knowing what happened to Jesus who tried to teach God's way, I still try to do what Jesus sent me to do, for I shudder when I read today's passage from Ezekiel where God tells Ezekiel "if you do not speak to the wicked person about their wickedness, I will hold you responsible for the consequences of his or her wrongdoing." I may have a lot to answer for because of things I didn't say or do and it frightens me.

Love is the motivation behind any form of fraternal correction. Paul tells us today: "owe nothing to anyone except to love one another." We don't go around finding fault with people because we enjoy it, we do it because we love them and we hate to see them doing things that will cause themselves harm, either spiritually (or physically). I include the idea of physical harm because a brother or sister may be destroying themselves by eating or drinking too much or smoking or getting no exercise or getting hooked on pornography or recreational drugs. The consequences of those things are addictive and destructive as we know.

Often our words of wisdom or encouragement, even offered in love, fall on deaf ears. In today's gospel, Jesus gives us one more way to help our brother or sister who is straying from the path of righteousness. Jesus encourages prayer for the person. As a matter of fact, even before we dare to offer advice or criticism to another, we should pray for the right words and then if we are pushed off or told to mind our own business, we should keep on praying for them. I think St. James summarized everything I have tried to say when he ended his epistle: "whoever brings back a sinner from the error of his way will save his (or her) soul from death and will cover a multitude of sins."

24th Sunday in Ordinary Time
September 11, 2005

HOMILY – (Sirach 27, 30 – 28, 7) (Mt. 18, 21–35) I welcome the classes of '43, '44, '45, and '46. I am grateful my friend and cousin, Fr. Don McCarthy, who was in the class of '43, could join us this evening to concelebrate the Mass. Today is Stewardship Sunday throughout the Archdiocese, and you probably wouldn't feel at home here if I didn't talk about money. Well, I do want to say something later on, but I'm not really ready to give a full-fledged Steward talk this weekend. We still have some things to talk about at Parish Pastoral Council before I can address that topic, so you're all lucky this year, because you won't hear a big sermon on money here and you'll probably miss it at your own parish. In place of that, I do have a little story to make you feel at home. One of our parishioners told me this story the other day. She does not want to be identified. She told me one Sunday Msgr. Schwartz was giving a very long sermon. She was three years old at the time and with the usual innocence of childhood she asked her mother in a fairly audible voice: "Is he going to talk all day?" The people around her didn't dare laugh, but a lot of them were smiling. She said he finished up his sermon rather quickly after that. I'll try not to do the same to everyone today. As George Burns said: "The secret of a good sermon is to have a good beginning and a good ending; and have the two as close together as possible."

The theme of our readings is on forgiveness. Reading the paper each day shows us what unforgiveness does to nations, as they keep trying to get revenge on one another for some real or imagined act of cruelty. Some of the battles between different peoples have roots that go back hundreds of years. Many still live by the ancient principle of "an eye for an eye and a tooth for a tooth." That rule was meant to keep a person from exacting more revenge than what was appropriate. In other words, if someone knocked out one of your teeth, you could only knock out one of theirs and no more! I couldn't find the exact quote, but I think it was Martin Luther King who said, if we all insisted on an eye for an eye and a tooth for a tooth, soon everyone in the world would be blind and toothless. In the Sermon on the Mount (Mt. 6, 38), Jesus told us that's no longer the rule we should live by. Today's parable illustrates his position of forgiveness. We can't hold on to hating and desire for revenge. We have to let go.

A couple of comments might help us get a feel for Jesus' parable. Our translation is very weak and does not give the full impact of what was going on. It spoke of "a huge amount" that a servant owed his king and then of "a much smaller amount" that was owed. The original version (in the Greek) says the man owed his king ten thousand talents. In today's money that would be about 2 or 3 billion dollars. In that society it was customary for people who couldn't pay off their debts to be sold into slavery. The king's generosity was beyond belief. The man whose debt was cancelled was owed (again looking at the original Greek) a hundred denarii. Translated into today's dollars, that's about $5000. It boggles our mind to think that anyone could be as selfish as the man in today's gospel. He was given so much and, in spite of the unbelievable example of generosity shown by his king, he hadn't learned how to be generous toward others.

Refusing to forgive is a form of anger, anger we will not let go of (or as the first reading describes it so poetically, anger that a person hugs tight). The man in the parable who refused to forgive his fellow servant may have been motivated by selfishness or pettiness or greed or by the refusal to let anyone take advantage of him. I think in most cases, however, when someone refuses to let go of their anger it is because of pride. We tell ourselves, when we are hurt by someone, we should not have been treated like that. No doubt we were treated badly, but we do more harm to ourselves than to anyone else when we keep that anger alive in us. It will only eat us up emotionally and maybe even physically. As a counselor I have seen what unforgiveness does to the individual who cannot let go of pain or hurt someone has caused them. Jesus' admonition to forgive is good not only spiritually but psychologically too. One of the people we often have difficulty forgiving is ourselves. We do something we are embarrassed about or ashamed of and we continue to beat ourselves up. I did it to myself for years and, as a result, I always felt a lot of depression. It took me a long time to realize my problem was pride (more accurately it was neurotic pride). Our pride tells us we should be better than we really are and when we fail, our pride comes down on us with a vengeance. Certainly we should keep working to improve ourselves and to learn from our mistakes (this is healthy pride), but we also need to accept the fact that we are not perfect. And beating ourselves up will not help us improve ourselves, it will only depress us. Often times people have complained to me in counseling or in confession "I don't feel as if God has forgiven me for what I did." I tell them, it's because they haven't forgiven themselves.

Obviously today's parable is about forgiveness, but there is another important element to it and that is that we must not forget how generous God has been to us. We celebrate God's goodness now as we continue on with our Mass thanking him for his mercy and love which is worth more than many billions of dollars. It's worth is infinite, because God's love is infinite. Amen.

25th Sunday in Ordinary Time
September 21, 2014

INTRODUCTION – (Isaiah 25, 6-9; Matthew 20, 1-16) God's people were in exile in Babylon, they were as depressed as anyone could possibly be. They had lost everything. They were sure they had even lost God's love because of their sinfulness. Today we hear God's prophet assure them it is never too late to return to the Lord. For God says: "my thoughts are not your thoughts nor are your ways my ways." Even though they knew they were not worthy of God's mercy, the prophet assures them if they turn back to God, they will have God's mercy. Why is God so generous and forgiving? It is his nature to be that way.

HOMILY – In today's parable, we certainly see that God's thoughts are not our thoughts, nor are our ways, God's ways. In today's parable, Jesus tells us this is what the kingdom of heaven is like and it doesn't sound as if the Lord and Master of the kingdom plays fair.

The landowner must have been very wealthy considering all the people he had to hire to harvest his vineyard. In a normal situation, the landowner would have sent his servant to go look for people to hire and also the servant would pay the workers at the end of the day. But here it is the landowner, the Lord himself who directs how things are to be in the kingdom. As was the custom of the day, a worker was hired early in the morning and paid at the end of the day (a 12- hour work day). A day's wage for an unskilled worker is often called by the Roman name, denarius. It was just barely enough to support a family for one day. The parable is shocking for us to hear because we tend to look at the story solely from a monetary perspective. We figure if one hour is worth X amount of money, then twelve hours should earn twelve times as much.

But the landowner was looking at things from two perspectives: justice and fairness on the one hand and mercy and generosity on the other. He was fair and just to those who worked all day (since they were paid what had been agreed upon) while he chose to be generous to those who would need enough money to feed their family that day or the next. But that explanation still leaves me with an unanswered question: why couldn't the master be just a little more generous to those who gave him a full day's work? Here's what I think is the answer to that question. Remember this is a parable of the kingdom. If the denarius is the reward given to all those who labored in the vineyard, then what does it represent for those who live and serve in God's kingdom? Most of us already know the denarius represents heaven. And heaven is not a silver coin. Heaven is perfect happiness, and it is forever. In other words, if you have heaven, you have everything and nothing more can be added to it to make it any greater or fuller. Some people work long and hard to gain this happiness, some don't work nearly as hard, they come in at the last minute, and when all have eventually attained heaven everyone will have all the happiness of which they are capable and it will last forever. So, although today's parable at first hearing seems unfair, we discover it is more than fair. It proclaims the wonderful generosity and mercy of God, which reaches out to all people, from those who were favored to have been first invited into the vineyard to those who just made it in at the last hour.

I cannot conclude without pointing out that there is a suggestion of the last judgment in today's parable. The fact that people came to work at different times throughout the day reminds us that there are many opportunities to enter the kingdom but such opportunities do not go on forever. Summer days are long, winter days are short, but every day lasts only so long and so does each person's life. Jesus always reminds us that the time is limited for us to respond to his invitation to be part of the kingdom. It was what Jesus announced when he first began to preach: "Repent, for the kingdom of heaven has drawn near." (Mt. 4,17) Amen.

26th Sunday in Ordinary Time
September 28, 2014

INTRODUCTION – (Ezekiel 18, 15-38; Matthew 21, 28-32) In 587 B.C. when the Babylonians conquered the Jews, tore down their Temple, burnt their cities and took the surviving Jews to Babylon as captives and slaves, the Jews concluded God was punishing them for the sins of their ancestors. They complained that God was not being fair to them. In our first reading we hear God tell them, through his prophet Ezekiel, it is their own sins that created the disaster they were suffering. Yet with

God the situation is never hopeless. They could always change their ways. We hear a similar message in today's gospel. If we have damaged our relationship with God, we can always turn things around.

HOMILY – In the preceding section of St. Matthew, we are told that Holy Week was beginning and Jesus had just arrived in Jerusalem in a triumphal manner, riding on a donkey with the people shouting after him "Hosanna, to the Son of David." These words mean: "Save us, Son of David." The people were bestowing on Jesus a kingly title, which could have caused a significant upheaval in the city of David where the Temple was and where the Romans were especially watchful for any signs of revolt or insurrection. After Jesus asserted his royal authority, he went into the Temple and drove out all those who were in the business of buying and selling animals for sacrifice and he overturned the tables of the money changers. Naturally, the religious leaders challenged Jesus. He was stepping on their turf. They demanded to know where he got the authority to do what he had just done. So Jesus challenges them with the parable you just heard in today's gospel.

The parable of the two sons shows us two children who must have been a handful for their father. Neither one responded obediently to the father's request for help in the vineyard. The first boy said "no" to the father - in that culture it was a real insult. But he felt guilty enough about it to go to work anyway in the vineyard. The second son answered "yes," but never followed through.

"Which of the two did his father's will?" is the main point in today's gospel. The son who said "no" at first, then changed his mind and went to work was the son who actually did what his father wanted. The other son was quite agreeable but was of no use to his father when it came to doing the job that needed to be done. Jesus is comparing the second son to the elders and chief priests in the way they responded to John the Baptist. According to Jesus, even the worst sinners (tax collectors and prostitutes) listened to John the Baptist and repented. The religious leaders did not change their sinful ways.

This is a theme of actually doing what God wants us to do - a theme that we find frequently in all the gospels, but especially in Matthew. Here are a few examples: Jesus says "not everyone who says to me 'Lord, Lord,' will enter the kingdom of heaven, but only the one who does the will of my Father in heaven." (Mt. 7, 21) At the end of the Sermon on the Mount, Jesus said: "everyone who listens to these words of mind and acts on them will be like a wise man who built his house on rock." (Mt. 7,24) By contrast, anyone who builds his life on any foundation other than God's word, Jesus calls a "fool." In a parable about a faithful servant, Jesus says when the master is out of town and unexpectedly returns to find his servant doing what he was supposed to be doing, that servant will be "blessed," while if he is not doing what he was supposed to do he will be severely punished. (Mt. 24,51). The famous parable of the Last Judgment is all about what we do for others that will gain heaven for us while we will find ourselves rejected by Jesus and thrown out of the kingdom because of what we did not do. (Mt. 25,31ff)

Our faith is not just a matter of saying the right words or celebrating proper ritual. Faith is no different than other parts of our life in this regard. Example: how well does it work in marriage if one partner is always agreeable but never follows through, or are your bosses or teachers pleased with you where you go to work or school when you talk a good talk but never accomplish what you are supposed to do? Our faith includes expressing ourselves in prayer and ritual (i.e. using fitting word) but it also requires that we put into action the message and the commands that Jesus has given us. If we haven't been living the way Jesus has taught us, it's never too late to change things around as the young man in the gospel shows us, the son who initially said "no" to his father, but then had a change of heart. Amen.

27th Sunday in Ordinary Time
October 5, 2014

INTRODUCTION – (Isaiah 5, 1-7; Matthew 21, 33-43) Most of us know how much work is involved in caring for a garden. Just imagine how much work is involved with setting up an entire vineyard. It is a full time occupation. In today's first reading, Isaiah the prophet, who lived in the 8th century BC, describes some of what was involved in caring for a vineyard. If we wonder why there needed to be a watchtower in the vineyard, it was needed, both day and night, to protect the grapes from thieves and predators, especially during harvest time. Apparently Isaiah was a musician as well as a talented poet. As he sang his song, we can imagine the shock his audience felt when they discovered they were the vineyard he was singing about. From history we know Isaiah's prophecy about the destruction of the vineyard literally proved to be true when first the Assyrians then later the Babylonians invaded the land of Israel and destroyed most of the cities, villages, homes and farms in Israel.

HOMILY – At this point in Matthew's gospel, Jesus is in Jerusalem at the Temple. Remember, the Temple was a large open area, enclosed by walls, but not a ceiling. The walls indicated where certain people were allowed to pray. The outside wall of the Temple formed the largest space about 4 football fields long and 2 1/2 football fields wide. Spaces were marked off for Gentiles and Jews, men and women, laity and priests. In the center of it all was the Holy Place and the Holy of Holies, where only the high priest could enter. Jesus had just cleansed the Temple of people buying and selling animals for sacrifice and of the money changers. Now he dares to teach in the Temple and even to heal sick people (who by law were not allowed in the Temple). It is the beginning of the last week of Jesus' earthly life, the week we call Holy Week. The elders and chief priests challenged him. They wanted to know who authorized him to do the things he was doing. Jesus answered their challenge by speaking three parables. The first of these three we heard last week, about the man who had two sons. He asked both of them to work in his vineyard. The first son said "no" but later regretted his response and went to work in the vineyard. The second son said "yes" to his father, but never went. Jesus compared the greatest sinners to the first son. They repented and reformed their lives through the preaching of John the Baptist. The elders and high priests, in other words, the Jewish religious leaders, were compared to the second son, who talked a good talk, but they didn't walk the path of holiness that John preached.

Today's parable is Jesus' second response to the Jewish leaders and next Sunday's is the third. They all tell us something about the kingdom. Today's parable is very easy to understand. The people of Israel are often compared to a vineyard in the Scriptures, and our first reading today is one of the best examples of that comparison. In the passage from Isaiah, the first reading, the complaint was with the grapes, they were too sour to be eaten or to be used for wine. In the gospel, notice that the problem is not with the grapes, but with those charged with the task of caring for the vineyard; in other words, the Jewish religious leaders. Throughout their 1000 year history, the leaders almost always rejected the teaching of the prophets. Often the prophets were put to death for doing what God had sent them to do. In the parable, the first two groups who were sent to the vineyard to obtain the fruit that was owed to the owner represent the prophets God sent. So the owner of the vineyard (that is, God) decided to send his son. It would be a huge offense (as well as a very stupid thing to do) if the workers rejected or harmed the son. It would be as grievous as if they were to do anything to the owner himself. But they thought they could get by with it. Instead, they lost everything they did have. Sometimes that happens to us when we get too greedy - one of the several lessons the story of Adam and Eve teaches us. Or as a friend of mine remarked when he lost a lot of money in the stock market: "you can be a bull or you can be a bear, but you can't be a pig."

The lesson on the kingdom: God looks for holiness among his people and he looks for those with authority, not only religious leaders but also parents and teachers, to lead God's people in that direction. It's a big responsibility. St. Paul, in today's second reading, gives us a good description of a holy life: a life of prayer, and thanksgiving, a life of trust in God's providence, a life of whatever is pure, honorable, just, gracious, a life of following the teachings and example of Jesus. Amen.

28th Sunday in Ordinary Time
October 12, 2014

INTRODUCTION – (Isaiah 25, 6-10a; Matthew 22, 1-14) Today's first reading and today's gospel give us a beautiful picture of what it is we're praying for when we say "thy will be done." God's will is for our complete and eternal happiness. Our gospel warns us, however, that in order to be part of his beautiful plan, we need to respond to the invitation he offers us. Our second reading is part of a thank you note St. Paul wrote to the Philippians for the money they sent him to help him most probably while he was in prison. The Philippian community was the only community that were thoughtful enough to offer him any support in his ministry.

HOMILY – Once more I wish to remind you that at this point in Matthew's gospel we are beginning the last week of Jesus' life here on earth. That week is known to us as Holy Week. As that week began, Jesus entered Jerusalem triumphantly, he went into the Temple and in anger drove out those carrying on business in the Temple, accusing them of having turned the Temple into a den of thieves. Then Jesus began teaching the crowd. People who were blind and lame were forbidden by law to enter the Temple, but when they entered and approached Jesus, instead of scolding them for entering, he healed them. The elders and priests confronted Jesus and demanded to know who gave him the authority to do what he was doing. He responded to them with three parables describing the kingdom of heaven. We have already heard two of those parables on the past two Sundays. Today we hear the third.

It is very similar to last Sunday's parable. The king in the parable represents God. A royal wedding at the time of Jesus would have been a spectacular event, as exciting and awesome as anything the ordinary person might get to experience in their entire lifetime. As the parable begins it is assumed that the invited guests would have accepted the invitation when it was first offered, but by the time of the great event, they all changed their mind.

They do not even offer an excuse, rather their rejection of the invitation and their violence toward the messengers from the king has the appearance of a rebellion on the part of the citizens against the king. And so the king's response is severe and he invites others to the banquet. The last part of the parable about not having a wedding garment reminds us if we are going to participate in this awesome event, we must come with the right attitude. Those judged worthy of the eternal banquet must come equipped with the deeds of an authentic Christian life. Their good deeds go with them as the book of Revelation tells us, and we should have some good deeds to bring with us.

I want to shift now to today's second reading. St. Paul is thanking the Philippian community for their goodness to him. He has a nice way of expressing his gratitude, as he says: "it was kind of you to share in my distress." In many ways the people of this parish share in the work of the parish, through sharing with us their time, talent and treasure. Today I want to talk about the treasure part of what you share. It is required of pastors that I do so. In a few days, I will send a letter out along with a finance report for our fiscal year July 1, 2013 to June 30, 2014. That same report is in today's bulletin, in case you do not get a letter. Financially it was not a year to brag about. We ended the year almost $40,000 in the red. However, God is good. A very kind and thoughtful person bailed us out by leaving St. Boniface Church a bequest for about $90,000 which just came to us a couple of weeks ago. God is good! That bequest will not only help us with our $40,000 deficit from our last fiscal year, but it will help us with sidewalk repair around the area of the school which was recently completed.

We had no big surprises this past year, and we do not anticipate any major repairs this current fiscal year.

What concerns me most is that already this fiscal year, since July 1, our collections are down almost $15,000. If they continue to drop at that rate, we will end the fiscal year about $60,000 in the red. I know that many of our parishioners come from outside of Northside and age and weather make it more difficult for them to be here. When you can't get here to Mass on a particular weekend, please, if you can, increase your contribution the next time you do come, or use direct deposit. We cannot close the church down when people are missing and we always have bills to pay.

We have an important ministry here at St. Boniface. You share in that ministry by your financial support. I am optimistic about our future. New people are going to be moving into Northside when a couple of building projects are finished and I am hopeful these should increase our attendance. But until we see that happen, St. Boniface has to rely on our faithful and generous parishioners. If you can share more generously, please do so. I know you are asking right now "what do you mean by more generously; give us a number." I figure it will take between a 5% and 10% increase in weekly income to bring us to where we need to be. I especially thank all of you for your support each Sunday and I pray you will help us to keep serving the Lord as we do. Remember, you will not outdo the Lord in generosity. You will be blessed by God more generously than you can imagine for your generous sharing in his work. Amen.

29th Sunday in Ordinary Time
October 19, 2014

INTRODUCTION – (Isaiah 45, 1.4-6; Matthew 22, 15-21) Roughly six hundred years before Christ, the

Babylonians (people living in what is Iraq today) conquered the Jews, destroyed everything they could and took most of the Jews to Babylon to be their slaves. Roughly 50 years later, the Persians (people living in what is Iran today) conquered the Babylonians. Cyrus was king of Persia at that time and he allowed the Jews to return to their own home in Israel. He even encouraged them to rebuild their temple to Yahweh. In today's first reading, we hear how the prophet saw God working through the Persian king, Cyrus. He calls Cyrus God's anointed. Cyrus, of course, claimed that he had overcome the Babylonians by his own strength and shrewdness. Isaiah said it was God who made it happen. We are reminded that even though God chooses to work through human agents, people who have a free will, God is still supreme and Lord throughout all of history and to him belongs all glory and honor.

HOMILY – In Matthew's gospel, we are in the last week of Jesus' life. The hostility toward Jesus had been rising rapidly after Jesus had cleansed the Temple. In today's gospel the Pharisees, who would have liked to see him dead, took an opportunity to attack him. They approached him along with the Herodians. This is significant. The Pharisees hated the Romans who were ruling Israel and the Herodians were favorable toward the Romans and cooperated with them. This left Jesus in trouble with one group or the other depending on how he answered the question about paying taxes to Caesar.

You might find it interesting to know that the tax in question was to be paid with a Roman coin which contained an image of the emperor and had on it the words: "Tiberius Caesar, august son of the divine Augustus, high priest." The Jews were against images to start with, and they would certainly have been against the reference to Caesar Augustus as divine. In spite of any objections, they may have had, however, they were able to produce a coin when Jesus didn't have one. By the way, the value of the tax was one denarius, owed by everyone between the ages of 12 or 14 to age 65. A denarius was one full day's pay for a laborer (things sure have changed.) There were other taxes, of course, taxes on what a farmer produced or what was transported, but there was a considerable amount of opposition among the Jews to this particular tax, not because it was excessive, I suspect, but more out of principle.

Jesus' answer was brilliant. Since the coin had the emperor's image engraved on it, it belonged to him. So give him what is his, but (and this is the important message in Jesus' answer) don't forget to give to God what belongs to God (love, prayer, sacrifice and obedience). In his answer Jesus allowed for limited cooperation with the Romans, but he did not allow for cheating God of what rightfully was owed to God.

I'm sure most of us find it much easier to cheat God than to cheat the government. If we cheat on our taxes, someone may soon notify us that we owe more than we claimed we owed. If we cheat on the time we owe God or cheat on following God's laws, no angel comes knocking, but it is our loss if we have not met our obligation to God, and what we have lost by cheating God can only be regained by a change of heart.

Without Jesus saying it, experience has taught us that the more we cheat God, the further we drift away from him. But Jesus has taught this in other places in the gospels. His answer achieved what he intended for it to achieve, to put the Pharisees in their place and to reveal their dishonest intentions.

30th Sunday in Ordinary Time
October 23, 2011

HOMILY – (Exodus 22:20-26; 1 Thes 1:5c-10; Matthew 22:34-40) When a woman teacher became engaged, one of her more experienced co-workers decided to give her some good advice. "Just remember, she said, the first ten years of marriage are the hardest." The younger teacher asked her co-worker how long she had been married. "Ten years," she answered. (from Reader's Digest, Laughter, the Best Medicine, pg. 161)

Our first reading and gospel present us with a very challenging topic: love. When we hear that word, we automatically think of romance, joy, and warm feelings. Sometimes it is; sometimes it's a matter of dedication, loyalty and commitment. Those who have matured in learning about love know that sometimes it's easy and sometimes it's hard work.

The Jewish leaders considered there were 613 precepts or commands in their law, the part of the Bible we call the "Old Testament." Jewish rabbis often debated which of these was the most important. So Jesus was asked what is the greatest. He states two, not one, as basic and central to everything else. The first is from the Book of Deuteronomy. It is part of a Scripture text that pious Jews recited twice a day. The second is from the Book of Leviticus. Putting these two together is original with Jesus and stresses Jesus' emphasis that true religion is more than a matter of external observance (which it is of course) but comes from the disposition of our hearts.

Now, this topic about the interior dispositions of our hearts deserves a whole homily by itself, but it will have to wait for another time.

Right now I want to stress the importance of the

external observance of God's law, that is, doing what God wants us to, even if we don't feel like it, even if our heart is not in it. I think many people in today's world think that love of God is just a matter of warm fuzzy thoughts and feelings about God, without much attention to our behavior as to whether we are doing what God wants us to do. For example, taking seriously the Commandment of keeping holy the Lord's day, taking any time for worship or serious prayer, many consider unnecessary. Jesus said in John's gospel: "if you love me you will keep my commandments." (Jn. 14:15) Notice which of these two commandments of love of God and neighbor Jesus said is the first and the greatest.

But the second is like it and we can't really love God whom we do not see if we do not love our neighbor whom we do see (1 John 4:20). There are almost an infinite number of ways we can love others: from common ordinary decency and friendliness to really putting ourselves out for those who are the most destitute as St. Francis or Mother Teresa did. This week, however, I would like to make a special reference to a man who had a great love for the people of Cincinnati: Carl Lindner. I have to mention him because he was such a special help to me while I was taking care of St. Joseph Church a few years ago. When I was assigned to pastor St. Joseph's Church temporarily (for three years), I discovered that Mr. Lindner had made a generous donation the previous year to St. Joe's at Christmas time. I got the idea that maybe with a special request, he would do more. How does a person get to see such an important figure as Carl Lindner? I didn't know how to reach him, but a good friend told me to go downtown to his office and ask to see him. So I stirred up the courage to do that. I went to his office building and asked the receptionist if I could talk with him. I was sent to a waiting room, offered something to drink, and waited about 15- 20 minutes and Carl Lindner came walking in with a couple of his staff members. He met with me for a little while, showed much interest in what I was doing and asked questions about St. Joe's Church and about its school. He offered to help me out and, subsequently, sent a donation 10 times what he had given in the past – which was considerable. Of course, I went back to thank him after we received it and every year after that he helped St. Joe and kept us out of the red. I felt this should be mentioned, because I'm sure he did lots of charity like that, things no one ever heard about. It was indeed a privilege to have known him. He was a Baptist, as most of you probably know, but he told me his mother was Catholic. I think that was why he was generous to Catholic organizations. One time when I went to thank him for his help, he said to me, "you know I help many people around the city and so few bother to say 'thanks.'" I was surprised to hear that, but I shouldn't have been surprised. It corresponds with the gospel story about Jesus healing the ten lepers, and only one returning to say "thanks."

That is why we are here today – to say "thanks" to God for all his goodness to us. The word "Eucharist" means "thanksgiving." We thank God for people like Carl Lindner as well as for people who have far fewer resources than he did but whose hearts are also generous and giving. I know many like that here at St. Boniface. Giving God thanks is an important part of our love for God. St. Paul tells us as much in Colossians: "Whatever you do, in word or deed, do everything in the name of the Lord Jesus, giving thanks to God the Father through him." (Colossians 3:17)

All Saints
November 1, 2005

INTRODUCTION – (Our first reading is from the book of Revelation (Rev. 7, 2–4. 9–14). The section just preceding today's passage described the end of the world. The sun became dark and the moon became red as blood and there was a great earthquake all over the earth. People tried to hide from all these terrible things and they asked: "Who can survive?" Today's reading answers the question: those who have followed Christ faithfully. And those who have followed Christ faithfully form a large crowd which no one could count. The number 144,000 is a symbolic number, symbolic of completion or perfection.

HOMILY – (Gospel: Matthew 5, 1–12a) Do you ever notice all the saints we have represented here at St. Boniface church? There is the Blessed Virgin altar and St. Joseph's altar with their statues. There are statues of St. Anthony, St. Rita, St. Teresa (aka, the Little Flower), St. Patrick and St. John Vianney (in the back). Someone asked where is the statue of St. Boniface. It's outside at the top of the front of the church. There are those in the stained glass windows: Sts. Martha and Mary, all the apostles, St. Boniface, St. Cecilia and St. Gregory the Great in the stained glass windows in the choir loft. There are thousands of others who are designated as "saints" in the Church. I have a book that lists 7000 "saints" and says a little bit about each one of them. Today's first reading tells us about a crowd so large that no one could count them. Who could count how many people there were who have lived holy lives and gone to heaven throughout these past 2000 years? I would have a hard time counting all the wonderful people I have known as a priest whom I'm sure God has welcomed into his kingdom.

We can learn a lot from all these holy people. Among them were people who died young and those who died old, those who were married, those who were single and those who were religious or priests. There were people from every walk of life, wealthy people and poor people and people in-between. Even though they had so many differences among them, they had certain things in common. They believed in God's love, they made loving God central in their own lives. Some even went so far as to suffer martyrdom rather than give up their commitment to God. They revered the Mass, the sacraments and the Scriptures. They loved others not just in an emotional sort of way but in a way so as to be of service and help to others. In today's feast, the Church not only wants us to remember all these holy people, but the Church puts them before us as guides on our own way to God. And it gives us the comfort of knowing that our relatives and friends who have gone before us and who have died in God's grace now enjoy the fullness of God's life and God's joy. Some of the saints, as we know, were not holy at all in their younger days, but they came to realize the error of their ways and turned their lives around, knowing God is always ready for us to turn back to him if we will.

God has called us all to a life of holiness. God has called us all to be saints. If we end up being pictured in some stained glass window in a church that might be nice, but what is really important is that we be among that great number in God's heavenly kingdom. St. John tells us in today's second reading (1 Jn 3, 1–3) that in God's love he has made us his children. We are not only called God's children but that's what we really are. We ask the Lord today to help us realize our dignity and our purpose to be God's children for all eternity with God in heaven.

All Souls
November 2, 2008

INTRODUCTION – (2 Maccabees 12:43-46: Romans 5:5-11, John 6:37-40) Our first reading, from the book of Maccabees, comes from about 100 years before Christ. At that time in history the Greeks were the dominant power and they were trying to get the Jews to abandon their faith and follow the beliefs of the pagans. Those who would not give in were persecuted and put to death. The loyal Jews fought back. In one of their battles, many Jews were killed. As they were being buried, it was found that they had small statues of pagan gods attached to their garments. These Jews were loyal to their Jewish beliefs, but they had, to some extent, given in to paganism. Just in case those pagan gods were real, they were carrying with them statues of pagan gods to give them protection. Their leader, Judas Maccabeus, took up a collection to send to Jerusalem for sacrifices to be offered up to the Lord for those people. He believed their hearts were, in general, in the right place, but for the weakness in their faith they had to be forgiven. In this piece of history from 100 B.C., we can see the beginnings of the belief that our prayers can help those who have died, a belief that is still part of our faith.

HOMILY – Praying for our deceased relatives and friends is what our feast of All Souls is about today. However, I had the hardest time getting started with today's homily. I kept putting it off. It's not as if I do not believe in praying for friends and relatives who have died. I do it all the time and it has been a tradition in the

Church from the beginning, and even before that as we heard in our first reading. I think the difficulty I had in developing my homily comes from two sources. First, many people don't like to hear about death and what might come afterwards. We know we can't avoid it, but my sense is that many people believe that if they don't think about it, it won't happen, at least not for a long time. My suspicion is that my father was that way. I constantly tried to get him to make a will but he never did. As a CPA he would have known it was a good idea. I think making a will would have made the prospect of his own death too concrete and too real for him to deal with. The second reason today's homily was hard was that I would have to talk about Purgatory. It's an idea that many Christians deny. I remember once I was helping a family prepare the liturgy for their deceased father and they insisted "absolutely no mention of Purgatory." It's as if it were a bad word. They wanted to think their father was perfect, I guess, and was already in heaven. Most of us would like to believe that our loved ones go straight to heaven when they die – period. If this were true, then they would not need our prayers. If they went to the other place, God forbid, our prayers would do them no good. The Church teaches, in every Mass we have for a person who died and in today's feast, that our prayers do help our relatives and friends who have left this world as they journey to eternal life.

Purgatory, among all the mysteries and beliefs of the Church is an extremely logical and comforting doctrine. It's logical if we ask ourselves how many of us think we will be perfect when we die. There may even be some who are perfect right now. I would ask them to identify themselves, but if they're perfect, they will also be too humble to do so. Even those who lived a good life may still have a little room for improvement, they may still not love God or others quite enough. That's where Purgatory comes in – it's an opportunity to grow into the most loving, most holy person we can possibly be. As a result we would then be filled with God's peace and joy and love to the fullest extent. Luther rejected the idea of Purgatory because of the abuse of indulgences at the time. Today, the concept of Purgatory has been rejected by many because of all the negative images of suffering and punishment that we grew up with. Actually, I think for the souls in Purgatory, happiness far outweighs the unhappiness. Their salvation is sure, they are more closely united with God than they had ever experienced before in their lives, they are on their way to the enjoyment of God's kingdom in the fullest possible way. But they're not there yet and that's the painful part.

If you read the book, "The Five People You Meet in Heaven," I think you get a good, practical image of Purgatory. It's not a religious book, it's very entertaining and it pictured for me what Purgatory might be like as we work out issues, regrets, hurts, conflicts, etc., that we might take with us when we die. To demonstrate that Purgatory makes so much sense, I think that those who deny Purgatory have had to find a substitute for it in their thinking about the next life. For many that substitute is reincarnation. In reincarnation a person supposedly keeps working for greater and greater purity and holiness until they are ready to be perfectly one with God. However, reincarnation comes from Hinduism. Actually a Hindu does not look forward to reincarnation because they don't want to have to pass through this world of pain and suffering one more time. I suspect the notion of reincarnation has been adopted by many Westerners, even Christians, because it fits our culture of "buy now, pay later." They figure they can live any way they want and can postpone having to pay any consequences. Our faith tells us, "now is the acceptable time, now is the day of salvation." God gives us what we need in this life to help us know him and serve him in this life. If we do not do it perfectly, Purgatory is there to finish the job. Today, we renew our faith in life after death. Today too we renew our belief in the power of prayer to help our loved ones, even those who are no longer among us, for in Christ they are still one with us. With Christ our great high priest, we offer now the greatest prayer there is, the Eucharist.

31st Sunday in Ordinary Time
October 30, 2005

INTRODUCTION – (Malachi 1, 14b–2, 2b. 8–10; Matthew 23, 1–12) Malachi was a prophet who lived about 400 years before Christ. He was definitely a fire and brimstone type prophet. Our reading begins with Malachi condemning the priests of his day for offering sacrifices unworthy of God. The usual sacrifice a person offered was an animal, usually sheep or oxen. People were bringing in animals for sacrifice that were blind, lame and sick – the kind of animals the owner wanted to get rid of anyway. The priest carried out the sacrifice and probably also had to be bribed in order to accept the animal since the law required that only perfect specimens be used in making a sacrifice to God. Malachi told them to offer that sick or blind animal as a gift to the governor and see if he would be pleased. The people were falling into sin, so Malachi condemned the priests for not teaching the people God's ways. One such thing the priests were telling the people was "everyone who does evil is good in the sight of the Lord, and he delights in them." It sounds like new age theology doesn't it? The last verse of the reading seems to be out of context as Malachi turns his focus to the people and chastises them for breaking God's covenant through sins of adultery, dishonesty and injustice. The reading prepares us for the gospel where Jesus condemns the Jewish leaders of his day.

HOMILY – Malachi and Jesus are dealing with the sinfulness of the religious leaders of their day. The priests in Malachi's day were offering unworthy sacrifices to God and neglecting to teach the people how God wanted them to live. In Jesus' day, the priests (also referred to as the Sadducees) received their share of condemnation from Jesus, but it seems the Pharisees and scholars of the law received the majority of Jesus' criticism. The Pharisees were not priests, but lay leaders, trained in leading the people in Scripture study and in liturgy. They were not all bad people. Remember Nichodemas and Joseph of Arimathea were Pharisees. So was Paul who at first persecuted the followers of Christ but later became the great apostle to the nations. Some of their membership, as we hear in today's gospel, were more interested in looking good rather than in being good. They were interested in using their position to bring glory upon themselves rather than to serve God's people and to lead them to give glory to God. At any time in history we can find leaders, religious or not, who were good leaders or who abused their position. It happens in religion, any religion, and it happens in all levels of society and business. And the abuse of power manifests itself in many ways. It is especially distressing when it happens among religious leaders. They, above all people, should be models of holy living. When I was growing up, the biggest scandals I would hear about were when priests or nuns thought they were little gods, thinking they should be treated as if they were on a pedestal and the world should bow to their demands. That pedestal has crumbled. The Church's voice of authority is simply ignored by many today. The scandal of priests abusing children and the way it was handled by the hierarchy has given the Church's authority a serious blow in our own day. We must remember that society needs authority, and the church needs authority so it does not degenerate into anarchy. I can understand the feelings of those who have walked away from the Church because of some people's abuse of power, but at the same time those who have walked away are missing a lot of good spiritual blessings because they have walked away. Jesus spoke very harshly of the punishment of those who cause scandal. It would be better for them if a great millstone were tied around their neck and they were thrown into the sea. Yet he also says to the people in today's gospel about the Pharisees: "do and observe all things whatsoever they tell you, but do not follow their example." It reminds me of a comment St. Theresa made about a spiritual director. She said she would rather have a learned priest as a spiritual director than a holy one. In other words, she figured she would get better guidance from one who knew what they were talking about than one who didn't. Ideally, of course, the best arrangement would be to have one who was both learned and holy. It's a goal I try to achieve in my own priesthood, but I know I do not always achieve it. I keep asking God's forgiveness for my failures. I am grateful to know that God is a merciful God. In turn I ask forgiveness of anyone I may have let down here at St. Boniface.

Many of you are in positions of authority too, maybe in your work, maybe as parents. Did you ever think that in your close relationships you exercise a kind of authority over others too, because in those relationships you are an influence on another person for better or for worse. Let us, in our prayers, remember all people who have positions of leadership in whatever field they serve that they may use their position to serve well. And may you who influence others in whatever way lead those under your care to know the God of love and to follow him in a sincere way. May you, in all your dealings, be both wise and holy. Amen.

32nd Sunday in Ordinary Time
November 6, 2005

INTRODUCTION – (Wisdom 6, 12–16; Matthew 25, 1–13) Wisdom and intelligence, to some extent, are connected with one another, but I've known intelligent people who were not always wise. Wisdom is more than intelligence. It is the ability to see the great mysteries of life in greater depth. It is gained from experience, and learning, and meditation, and it is practical as we hear Jesus explain it in today's gospel. When I read the paper about those who are fighting against the teaching that the universe could have come about by "intelligent design," I wonder if it's wisdom that they are missing out on. In spite of mysteries we can't solve, they can't conceive the possibility that there is some intelligence behind all that exists in our universe. Our first reading tells us wisdom is available for anyone who seeks it with honesty and openness. But those who find the search for wisdom too much trouble will be deprived of it.

HOMILY – A wedding is a big deal for us today, but after months of preparation, it's over in just a few hours. At the time of Jesus it was really a big deal. They would celebrate for days. And there was no such thing as saying the wedding will be at such and such a place at 6:30 in the evening. According to custom the groom would go to the bride's house to negotiate with the bride's father and then the groom would bring the bride with him to his home and the celebrating would begin. On their approach to the home of the husband, the couple were to be met by ten virgins carrying lamps. (Street lights weren't invented yet, you know.) Perhaps the groom was doing a little partying on his own before he went to claim his bride from her father, or maybe the groom and the father did a lot of dickering over what possessions the bride would bring with her when she left. At any rate no one worried too much about the time, especially since the celebration would last for a few days. The wise virgins were smart enough to prepare for whatever might happen. The foolish ones used no foresight at all. That's part of wisdom: foresight, thinking ahead, considering what could happen if we take or do not take a certain course of action, being prepared. Jesus applies his lesson to eternal life. We're only in this life for a short time. "Our citizenship is in heaven," St. Paul tells us. We're just tourists here, no matter what country or city we call home. Everything is temporary. Jesus tells us the wise person thinks ahead, they know some day they will have to meet their maker and they are practical. They make sure that they will be prepared when the Lord shows up on their doorstep. We can't interpret the oil in the story too literally. If we think of it as a material object that could be shared, we're going to think how selfish of those five wise virgins. But it is something symbolic that is intangible, something that cannot be given to someone else. It is something that we have worked for like a loving relationship with God or the good works we have done or the wisdom we have gained through prayer and meditation. The person we have come to be through God's grace can't just be put into a bottle and given to someone else. When I read about these five wise women, I can't help mentioning two wise women I knew well who have met the bridegroom this past week. The first was Sister Joann, our principal here at St. Boniface for 18 years. As a dedicated Sister of Charity for 55 years, almost all of that time serving as a teacher or a principal, I can only marvel how many lives she has touched and how many people's lives have been blessed because of her. Her lamp was filled with good works. The other wise woman I am thinking of is my step-mother. When I was 14 years old, the oldest of five, my mother died. My dad had five children to raise. Within a few months, Rosella came into our lives. She and my father were soon married and Rosella took care of us, until we had to start taking care of her. For the past three years the Little Sisters of the Poor took over caring for her and they did a marvelous job. After 52 years as our step-mother, we said goodbye to her this week as God took her. She was a wise lady, always putting God first. Her day always began with daily Mass when she was able to get to church. At the Little Sisters she was able to get to daily Mass, although at 95 she sometimes slept through it. She always taught us, and her step grandchildren, to keep God first too. I would visit her every week and whenever I was leaving she would tell me: "If you don't see me next week, I'm on my way to heaven." She was totally at peace with herself, her God and all people she knew. Her lamp was filled with good works.

Our gospel is a little frightening today. It tells us about ten women, five of whom were prudent and wise and five who lost out on a grand time because they were not. The frightening thing was, they almost made it. There's a saying "almost doesn't count, except in horseshoes." Our eternal happiness is too important to leave to "almost." God wants us to be happy. He wants us to spend eternity with him. And for that we must give him our love. And love isn't a matter of almost. A couple in love do not say to one another "I almost love you." Love is total. The only way we'll be totally happy is to totally love the God who is love. Amen.

33rd Sunday in Ordinary Time
November 16, 2014

INTRODUCTION – (Proverbs 31: 10-13,19-20,30-31; 1 Thes. 5: 1-6; Matthew 25: 14-30)Our first reading from the Book of Proverbs was written in the wisdom tradition of the Old Testament. Other books in the wisdom tradition include the Book of Wisdom, Ecclesiastes (aka Qoheleth), Song of Songs, Sirach and Job. This collection of writings was meant to help people search for and find wisdom. Today's passage describes the ideal wife, one who exemplifies all the elements of wisdom. The passage is meant to compliment the gospel which gives us a parable about three servants who received enormous gifts from their master; two of the three used their gift wisely, the third did not.

HOMILY – The gospel of Matthew contains five major speeches of Jesus. The first of those speeches is the Sermon on the Mount. There are four other lengthy teachings of Jesus. Today's gospel is from the last major speech and it is called the Eschatological Discourse. Eschatological means Jesus is talking to us about the last things: the end of the world, the coming of the Son of Man on the last day, the last judgment, and the arrival of God's kingdom in its fullness.

That is the context for today's gospel. The return of the master (the Lord) represents the last judgment when the Lord will ask each of us "what did you do with the gifts I have given you?" The gifts that had been given to the servants were talents, which was a certain weight of gold or silver. Commentators cannot give a clear idea of what a talent was worth. I've seen it valued as anything from $1000 to a million dollars. Whatever, for simple people who were usually paid each day just enough to survive the next day, a talent was a lot of money. It might be interesting to mention it was through familiarity with this word talent in today's gospel that in the Middle Ages the word talent came to mean a special gift of being able to do something well.

Note, the master does not tell his servants what to do with the money. He obviously expects them to follow the example he had always shown them, to use the time they had as they waited for his return, to increase what they had been given. I probably would not have been too hard on the third servant who buried his money. Burying the money was a prudent thing, so it would not be found or stolen. The master, however, in his wisdom saw it as laziness.

There is one thing about the money that is important but which we don't notice until the end of the parable. The master was giving the money to his servants, not in order to get it back, but as a personal gift to each of them. Apparently, they didn't know that until the master said "take the talent from him (the one who buried it) and give it to the one with the ten talents." God doesn't want back the gifts he gives us; he wants us to use them to help others and to increase them in ourselves. He doesn't want us to bury them in the ground until we see our end is near and then we can dig them up so as to return them to the Lord.

We've been told many times that using the gifts we've been given, whatever they might be, will help us be successful in this life. Jesus wants us to be successful spiritually by using the spiritual gifts we've been given, the Scriptures, the Sacraments, the time we can use for prayer, being good to others, and the inspiration of the Holy Spirit. If we do nothing with the graces and opportunities God has given us, it will not be a good thing. There will be more next week about the Last Judgment - how those who put their gifts and talents to good use were happy they did, while those who held on to them just for themselves ended up deeply regretting it. Amen.

Christ the King
November 23, 2014

INTRODUCTION - (Ezekiel 34, 11-12. 15-17; 1 Cor. 15, 20-26,28; Matthew 25, 31-46) Today we honor Christ as our King. Our scripture readings do not picture him as a typical king. In our first reading, Ezekiel, the prophet, pictures God as a shepherd. God is distressed with the shepherds of his people; i.e., the kings and religious leaders. They led God's people away from God and to eventual disaster at the time of the Babylonian invasion. God said he himself would lead them rightly. We see this prophecy perfectly fulfilled in Jesus. In our second reading, the whole 15th chapter from Paul's First Letter to the Corinthians, from which our reading is taken, is on the topic of the resurrection. Paul tells us the risen Jesus will reign until evil in every form has been destroyed. Then Jesus will turn the kingdom over to the Father. In the gospel Jesus is pictured as a judge, a judge who judges us on how we behave toward the lowly and the poor. Thus we have three images of Christ the King: a shepherd, the risen Lord and the judge of all nations.

HOMILY – In Matthew's gospel, Jesus' first major sermon is the Sermon on the Mount. The sermon begins with the beatitudes, one of which is: "blessed are the merciful, for they will obtain mercy." Today's gospel is the last of Jesus' major sermons in Matthew, and it dramatically portrays what Jesus means by "blessed are the merciful."

Today's gospel is one of the best known of Jesus' parables. It tells us, first of all, that at the end of time there will be only two kingdoms: the kingdom of God where there will be happiness beyond anything we can imagine and there will be the kingdom of Satan where there will be endless remorse and suffering. Notice that we're the ones who make the decision as to which kingdom we will belong - we make that choice not by what we say but by the way we live. Karma is a reality.

The parable tells us about who Jesus is. He is the Son of Man, a mysterious heavenly being to whom God grants dominion, glory and kingship (Daniel 7,14). Jesus has God for his Father (Mt. 25,34) He is called "king," which indicates Messiah and Son of David in Matthew and is also called "Lord" (Mt. 25, 37). He is both judge and shepherd. Jesus' identity was hidden, except in the things that he did (forgiving sins, interpreting the Law, healing the sick, raising the dead and various other miracles), but here Jesus appears in all his glory.

The usual interpretation of today's gospel is that "all the nations" need to respond to the needs of people experiencing some form of distress, "these least brothers of mine." A person might ask, "What about going to Church on Sunday?" What about the other commandments? Aren't those things important? Of course they are. Jesus did say the first and greatest commandment is to love God with our whole heart and soul and mind and strength. Loving God involves more than giving a sandwich to a hungry person or giving a cup of water to a thirsty person. It does include that, but it also includes prayer and worship and keeping the commandments. "If you love me you will keep my commandments," Jesus told his disciples at the Last Supper.

One commentator, Fr. Daniel Harrington, had a different interpretation for today's gospel. His interpretation asks what do these two phrases mean: "all the nations," and "these least brothers of mine." He points out when Matthew speaks of all the nations in other places in his gospel, he is speaking of the Gentiles - those who are not Jewish or are not identified as the people of God. When he speaks of the least of his brothers he is talking about Christian missionaries or ordinary Christians. If these translations are correct, the passage is about Jesus judging Gentiles and how they treated Christian missionaries or ordinary Christians. Is this an important question for us? It certainly is a question frequently asked these days: "Can non-Christians get into heaven?" According to Fr. Harrington, this is one of the very few texts in Scripture that deals with the salvation of non-Christians and how they can be saved. They are saved by the way they treat Christian missionaries or ordinary Christians. Why is that so? Because such acts of kindness are done for Christ himself. "Whoever receives you, receives me and whoever receives me, receives him who sent me," Jesus said to his disciples when he sent them out to preach. Well then, does the parable teach us anything about what is expected of us - we who are Christians. We have lots of instructions, the Scriptures, the Sacraments, the Catechism, the lives of saints who are great examples of love of others. If Gentiles are expected to show kindness for God's people, how much more are we expected to show kindness to others.

One last thought about this gospel. It gave me some insight into why heaven will be such a happy place. Consider the kind of people God invites into his kingdom - people who care about others, not people whose care is only about themselves. If you were surrounded only by people who were caring and loving people, wouldn't life be much more pleasant? Amen.

From *Rita Robinson Ring,*
Co-founder of Shepherds of Christ

God has chosen us, we are to turn to Christ with greater generosity, and as baptized Christians to grow in our knowing and loving capacity.

God has put His handprint on us in baptism giving to us the virtues of faith, hope and love. These are theological virtues. We must pray to God for the increase in these virtues and we respond to the grace He outpours to us. In praying for the increase in faith we can see more and more the vision of the Heavenly Father. We can hope for our eternal salvation and help spread that hope in our lives to others and we can share more deeply in God's loving activity – loving more supernaturally as we cooperate by responding to the gifts given by God of greater faith, hope and love.

God is with us, God wants us to spread the good news, to turn toward Him in loving union performing good acts according to His will.

Fr. Joe's book teaches us about love and life in God. Fr. Joe's book teaches us about the gift of the Mass and the Church, and about salvation history. We live more every day according to the scriptures in peace, love and joy. We know Jesus, we love Him. He is operating in us.

We all seek happiness – Happiness is found in God –

In reading the weekly scriptures and reading Fr. Joe's homily – God's loving self-communication to us will grow in our lives – as we respond in love to Him.

This book and the scripture come alive in our lives every Sunday after we read the scriptures and Fr. Joe's homily before Mass.

God communicates His own life through grace and man in return gives himself to God and his fellowman in loving service.

Happiness comes to us in dying to those ways not likened to God and rising in the spiritual life in that image and likeness of Christ.

We love Fr. Joe's jokes that help us to clear our minds and laugh and listen.

He told me of a little boy who was drawing a picture in art class and the teacher said "Who is this?" And the little boy said, "It is God."

The teacher said, "Nobody knows what God looks like." The little boy said, "When I get done – they will know."

In baptism we have been given a sharing in God's life with this elevated knowing and loving capacity.

It is up to us to pray to God for the grace to grow to know and love Him more – to be more and more likened to God.

In the pages of Fr. Joe's homilies we learn more and more about God, about loving God and loving others as ourselves – God is love – God is the source of love – We are to Respond to God's love.

Excerpt from *Response to God's Love* by Fr. Edward Carter, S.J.

"... In reference to Christianity, God himself is the ultimate mystery. Radically, God is completely other and transcendent, hidden from man in his inner life, unless he chooses to reveal himself. Let us briefly look at this inner life of God.

The Father, in a perfect act of self-expression, in a perfect act of knowing, generates his son. The

Son, the Word, is, then, the immanent expression of God's fullness, the reflection of the Father. Likewise, from all eternity, the Father and the Son bring forth the Holy Spirit in a perfect act of loving.

At the destined moment in human history, God's self-expression, the Word, immersed himself into man's world. God's inner self-expression now had also become God's outer self-expression. Consequently, the mystery of God becomes the mystery of Christ. In Christ, God tells us about himself, about his inner life, about his plan of creation and redemption. He tells us how Father, Son, and Holy Spirit desire to dwell within us in the most intimate fashion, how they wish to share with us their own life through grace. All this he has accomplished and does accomplish through Christ. St. Paul tells us: "I became a minister of this Church through the commission God gave me to preach among you his word in its fullness, that mystery hidden from ages and generations past but now revealed to his holy ones. God has willed to make known to them the glory beyond price which this mystery brings to the Gentiles — the mystery of Christ in you, your hope of glory. This is the Christ we proclaim while we admonish all men and teach them in the full measure of wisdom, hoping to make every man complete in Christ" (Col 1:25-28)."

Excerpts from *Guiding Light – Feed My Soul*

p. 111 When Jesus said the two greatest commandments were about love: love of God and love of neighbor, the Jewish scholar asked Jesus another question: "And who is my neighbor?" You might recall that there was great animosity between Jews and Samaritans, so in introducing a Samaritan into the story, Jesus shows us "neighbor" could be anyone, even someone we despise.

p. 51 The conversation Jesus had about tragic events at the beginning of today's gospel was interesting. Sometimes people think when something bad happens to someone it is God's punishment. Jesus said that's not always true. He does not try to explain suffering here, but he is telling us not to be complacent, which we sometimes are. We can't think "well, if nothing bad is happening to me, it must be because I am so good." He tells us we all need to repent, i.e., to work to be better than we are.

pp. 29-30 As we celebrate Jesus' baptism, may we at the same time celebrate our own. May we rejoice in God's gift of love and life given to us, and may we live up to the high dignity with which God has blessed us.

A Priest Is a Gift from God

by Rita Ring

A Song from Jesus

by Rita Ring

REFRAIN

I come to you with great-est love, I am your lov-ing Sav-ior. I am your God, I died for you, I come to you this day.

VERSES

1. You are My pre-cious lit-tle one, I love you oh so dear-ly. Come close to Me, My lit-tle one, I loved you to My death.
2. Reach out to Me and do not fear, I want to be so close to you. You are My child, My pre-cious one, I love you ten-der-ly.

I Love You Jesus

by Rita Ring

VERSES

1. Oh Burn-ing Heart, Oh Love di - vine, how
2. I can-not say. There are not words to
3. Your ten - der Heart, Oh how it beats for

sweet You are to me. I see the host, I
say what my heart feels. I love You so, I
love of each this day. I want to give You

know You're here to love and care for me.
scarce can breathe when You come in - to me.
all my love, sur - ren - der to - tal - ly.

REFRAIN

I know Your love a lit - tle now, so

dear You are to me. Come give me life, a -

bun - dant life, I thirst to be with Thee.

The Rosary Song

by Rita Rin

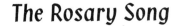

REFRAIN

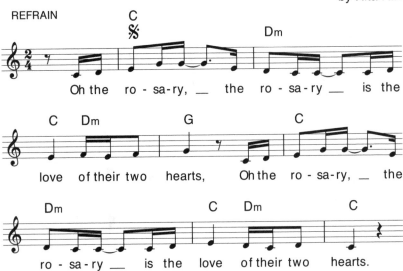

Oh the ro-sa-ry, __ the ro-sa-ry __ is the

love of their two hearts, Oh the ro-sa-ry, __ the

ro-sa-ry __ is the love of their two hearts.

VERSES 1-4

1. A - ve Ma - ri - a, A - ve Ma - ri - a. Oh the
2. Je - sus we love You, Ma - ry we love__ you. Oh the
3. This is her peace plan, Chil-dren must pray__ it. Oh the
4. We turn to Ma - ry, She is the Queen of Peace. Oh the

VERSE 5

No left hand

5. Oh Sa-cred Heart di - vine, Oh heart of Ma-ry pure,

A - ve Ma - ri - a, We love to pray it! Oh the

"This is My Body, This is My Blood."

Prayer Before the
Holy Sacrifice of the Mass

Let me be a holy sacrifice and unite with God in the sacrament of His greatest love.

I want to be one in Him in this act of love, where He gives Himself to me and I give myself as a sacrifice to Him. Let me be a holy sacrifice as I become one with Him in this my act of greatest love to Him.

Let me unite with Him more, that I may more deeply love Him. May I help make reparation to His adorable Heart and the heart of His Mother, Mary. With greatest love, I offer myself to You and pray that You will accept my sacrifice of greatest love. I give myself to You and unite in Your gift of Yourself to me. Come and possess my soul.

Cleanse me, strengthen me, heal me. Dear Holy Spirit act in the heart of Mary to make me more and more like Jesus.

Father, I offer this my sacrifice, myself united to Jesus in the Holy Spirit to You. Help me to love God more deeply in this act of my greatest love.

Give me the grace to grow in my knowledge, love and service of You and for this to be my greatest participation in the Mass. Give me the greatest graces to love You so deeply in this Mass, You who are so worthy of my love.

– *Mass Book*, December 27, 1995

Shepherds of Christ Associates

PRAYER MANUAL

Shepherds of Christ Publications
China, Indiana

Imprimi Potest: Rev. Bradley M. Schaeffer, S.J.
           Provincial
           Chicago Province, The Society of Jesus
Imprimatur: Most Rev. Carl K. Moeddel
           Auxiliary Bishop
           Archdiocese of Cincinnati

The Shepherds of Christ Associates Prayer Manual is published by
Shepherds of Christ Publications, an arm of Shepherds of Christ Ministries,
P.O. Box 627 Madison (China), Indiana 47250 USA.

Founder, Shepherds of Christ Ministries:
           Father Edward J. Carter, S.J.

For more information contact:
           Shepherds of Christ Associates
           P.O. Box 627
           Madison (China), Indiana 47250- USA
           Tel. 812-273-8405
           Toll Free: 1-888-211-3041
           Fax 812-273-3182

First Printing, September 1994
Second Printing, November 1994
Third Printing, November 1995
Fourth Printing, March 1996

Chapter Meeting
Prayer Format

The prayer format below should be followed at chapter meetings of *Shepherds of Christ Associates*. All prayers, not just those said specifically for priests, should include the intention of praying for all the needs of priests the world over.

1. **Hymns.** Hymns may be sung at any point of the prayer part of the meeting.

2. **Holy Spirit Prayer.** Come, Holy Spirit, almighty Sanctifier, God of love, who filled the Virgin Mary with grace, who wonderfully changed the hearts of the apostles, who endowed all Your martyrs with miraculous courage, come and sanctify us. Enlighten our minds, strengthen our wills, purify our consciences, rectify our judgment, set our hearts on fire, and preserve us from the misfortunes of resisting Your inspirations. Amen.

3. **The Rosary.**

4. **Salve Regina.** "Hail Holy Queen, Mother of mercy, our life, our sweetness, and our hope. To you do we cry, poor banished children of Eve. To you do we send up our sighs, our mourning, our weeping in this vale of tears. Turn, then, most gracious advocate, your eyes of mercy toward us and after this, our exile, show unto us the blessed fruit of your womb, Jesus, O clement, O loving, O sweet Virgin Mary. Amen."

5. **The Memorare.** "Remember, O most gracious Virgin Mary, that never was it known that anyone who fled to your protection, implored your help, or sought your intercession was left unaided. Inspired by this confidence, I fly unto you, O Virgin of virgins, my

Mother. To you I come, before you I stand, sinful and sorrowful. O Mother of the Word Incarnate, despise not my petitions, but, in your mercy, hear and answer me. Amen."

6. **Seven Hail Marys in honor of the Seven Sorrows of Mary.** Mary has promised very special graces to those who do this on a daily basis. Included in the promises of Our Lady for those who practice this devotion is her pledge to give special assistance at the hour of death, including the sight of her face. The seven sorrows are:

(1) The first sorrow: the prophecy of Simeon (Hail Mary).

(2) The second sorrow: the flight into Egypt (Hail Mary).

(3) The third sorrow: the loss of the Child Jesus in the temple (Hail Mary).

(4) The fourth sorrow: Jesus and Mary meet on the way to the cross (Hail Mary).

(5) The fifth sorrow: Jesus dies on the cross (Hail Mary).

(6) The sixth sorrow: Jesus is taken down from the cross and laid in Mary's arms (Hail Mary).

(7) The seventh sorrow: the burial of Jesus (Hail Mary).

7. **Litany of the Blessed Virgin Mary.**
   Lord, have mercy on us.
   Christ, have mercy on us.
   Lord, have mercy on us. Christ, hear us.
   Christ, graciously hear us.
   God, the Father of heaven, *have mercy on us.*
   God, the Son, Redeemer of the world,
   have mercy on us.
   God, the Holy Spirit, *have mercy on us.*

Holy Trinity, one God, *have mercy on us.*
Holy Mary, *pray for us* (repeat after each invocation).
Holy Mother of God,
Holy Virgin of virgins,
Mother of Christ,
Mother of the Church,
Mother of divine grace,
Mother most pure,
Mother most chaste,
Mother inviolate,
Mother undefiled,
Mother most amiable,
Mother most admirable,
Mother of good counsel,
Mother of our Creator,
Mother of our Savior,
Virgin most prudent,
Virgin most venerable,
Virgin most renowned,
Virgin most powerful,
Virgin most merciful,
Virgin most faithful,
Mirror of justice,
Seat of wisdom,
Cause of our joy,
Spiritual vessel,
Vessel of honor,
Singular vessel of devotion,
Mystical rose,
Tower of David,
Tower of ivory,
House of gold,
Ark of the Covenant,
Gate of heaven,

Morning star,
Health of the sick,
Refuge of sinners,
Comforter of the afflicted,
Help of Christians,
Queen of angels,
Queen of patriarchs,
Queen of prophets,
Queen of apostles,
Queen of martyrs,
Queen of confessors,
Queen of virgins,
Queen of all saints,
Queen conceived without original sin,
Queen assumed into heaven,
Queen of the most holy rosary,
Queen of families,
Queen of peace,
Lamb of God, who take away the sins of the world,
spare us, O Lord.
Lamb of God, who take away the sins of the world,
graciously hear us, O Lord.
Lamb of God, who take away the sins of the world,
have mercy on us.
Pray for us, O holy Mother of God,
*that we may be made worthy of the promises of
Christ.*

Let us pray: Grant, we beseech You, O Lord God, that we Your servants may enjoy perpetual health of mind and body and, by the glorious intercession of the blessed Mary, ever virgin, be delivered from present sorrow, and obtain eternal joy. Through Christ our Lord. Amen.

We fly to your patronage, O holy Mother of God. Despise not our petitions in our necessities, but deliver us always from all dangers, O glorious and blessed Virgin. Amen.

8. **Prayer to St. Joseph.** St. Joseph, guardian of Jesus and chaste spouse of Mary, you passed your life in perfect fulfillment of duty. You supported the Holy Family of Nazareth with the work of your hands. Kindly protect those who trustingly turn to you. You know their aspirations, their hardships, their hopes; and they turn to you because they know you will understand and protect them. You too have known trial, labor, and weariness. But, even amid the worries of material life, your soul was filled with deep peace and sang out in true joy through intimacy with the Son of God entrusted to you, and with Mary, His tender Mother. Amen.

— *(Pope John XXIII)*

9. **Litany of the Sacred Heart, promises of the Sacred Heart.**
Lord, have mercy on us.
Christ, have mercy on us.
Lord, have mercy on us. Christ, hear us.
Christ, graciously hear us.
God the Father of heaven,
have mercy on us (repeat after each invocation).
God the Son, Redeemer of the world,
God the Holy Spirit,
Holy Trinity, one God,
Heart of Jesus, Son of the eternal Father,
Heart of Jesus, formed by the Holy Spirit in the womb of the Virgin Mother,
Heart of Jesus, substantially united to the Word of God,
Heart of Jesus, of infinite majesty,

Heart of Jesus, sacred temple of God,
Heart of Jesus, tabernacle of the Most High,
Heart of Jesus, house of God and gate of heaven,
Heart of Jesus, burning furnace of charity,
Heart of Jesus, abode of justice and love,
Heart of Jesus, full of goodness and love,
Heart of Jesus, abyss of all virtues,
Heart of Jesus, most worthy of all praise,
Heart of Jesus, king and center of all hearts,
Heart of Jesus, in whom are all the treasures of
    wisdom and knowledge,
Heart of Jesus, in whom dwells the fullness of
    divinity,
Heart of Jesus, in whom the Father is well pleased,
Heart of Jesus, of whose fullness we have all
    received,
Heart of Jesus, desire of the everlasting hills,
Heart of Jesus, patient and most merciful,
Heart of Jesus, enriching all who invoke You,
Heart of Jesus, fountain of life and holiness,
Heart of Jesus, propitiation for our sins,
Heart of Jesus, loaded down with opprobrium,
Heart of Jesus, bruised for our offenses,
Heart of Jesus, obedient even to death,
Heart of Jesus, pierced with a lance,
Heart of Jesus, source of all consolation,
Heart of Jesus, our life and reconciliation,
Heart of Jesus, victim of sin,
Heart of Jesus, salvation of those who hope in You,
Heart of Jesus, hope of those who die in You,
Heart of Jesus, delight of all the saints,
Lamb of God, Who take away the sins of the world,
    spare us, O Lord.
Lamb of God, Who take away the sins of the world,

graciously hear us, O Lord.
Lamb of God, Who take away the sins of the world,
have mercy on us.
Jesus, meek and humble of heart,
make our hearts like unto Yours.

Let us pray: O almighty and eternal God, look upon the Heart of Your dearly beloved Son and upon the praise and satisfaction He offers You in behalf of sinners and, being appeased, grant pardon to those who seek Your mercy, in the name of the same Jesus Christ, Your Son, Who lives and reigns with You, in the unity of the Holy Spirit, world without end. Amen.

Promises of Our Lord to those devoted to His Sacred Heart (these should be read by the prayer leader):

(1) I will give them all the graces necessary in their state of life.
(2) I will establish peace in their homes.
(3) I will comfort them in all their afflictions.
(4) I will be their refuge during life and above all in death.
(5) I will bestow a large blessing on all their under-takings.
(6) Sinners shall find in My Heart the source and the infinite ocean of mercy.
(7) Tepid souls shall grow fervent.
(8) Fervent souls shall quickly mount to high perfection.
(9) I will bless every place where a picture of My Heart shall be set up and honored.
(10) I will give to priests the gift of touching the most hardened hearts.
(11) Those who promote this devotion shall have their names written in My Heart, never to be blotted out.

(12) I promise you in the excessive mercy of My Heart that My all-powerful love will grant to all those who communicate on the first Friday in nine consecutive months the grace of final penitence; they shall not die in My disgrace nor without receiving their sacraments; My divine Heart shall be their safe refuge in this last moment.

10. **Prayer for Priests.** "Lord Jesus, Chief Shepherd of the Flock, we pray that in the great love and mercy of Your Sacred Heart You attend to all the needs of Your priest-shepherds throughout the world. We ask that You draw back to Your Heart all those priests who have seriously strayed from Your path, that You rekindle the desire for holiness in the hearts of those priests who have become lukewarm, and that You continue to give Your fervent priests the desire for the highest holiness. United with Your Heart and Mary's Heart, we ask that You take this petition to Your heavenly Father in the unity of the Holy Spirit. Amen."

11. **Prayer for all members of the Shepherds of Christ Associates.** "Dear Jesus, we ask Your special blessings on all members of Shepherds of Christ Associates. Continue to enlighten them regarding the very special privilege and responsibility you have given them as members of Your movement, Shepherds of Christ Associates. Draw them ever closer to Your Heart and to Your Mother's Heart. Allow them to more and more realize the great and special love of Your Hearts for each of them as unique individuals. Give them the grace to respond to Your love and Mary's love with an increased love of their own. As they dwell in Your Heart and Mary's Heart, abundantly care for all their needs and those of their loved ones. We make our

prayer through You to the Father, in the Holy Spirit, with Mary our Mother at our side. Amen."

12. **Prayer for the spiritual and financial success of the priestly newsletter.** "Father, we ask Your special blessings upon the priestly newsletter, Shepherds of Christ. We ask that You open the priest-readers to the graces You wish to give them through this chosen instrument of Your Son. We also ask that You provide for the financial needs of the newsletter and the Shepherds of Christ Associates. We make our prayer through Jesus, in the Holy Spirit, with Mary at our side. Amen."

13. **Prayer for all members of the human family.** "Heavenly Father, we ask Your blessings on all Your children the world over. Attend to all their needs. We ask Your special assistance for all those marginalized people, all those who are so neglected and forgotten. United with our Mother Mary, we make this petition to You through Jesus and in the Holy Spirit. Amen."

14. **Prayer to St. Michael and our Guardian Angels:** "St. Michael the Archangel, defend us in battle. Be our safeguard against the wickedness and snares of the devil. May God rebuke him, we humbly pray, and do thou, O prince of the heavenly hosts, by the power of God, cast into hell Satan and all the other evil spirits who prowl about the world seeking the ruin of souls. Amen."

"Angel of God, my guardian dear, to whom God's love commits me here, ever this day be at my side, to light and guard, to rule and guide. Amen."

15. **Pause for silent, personal prayer.** This should last at least five minutes.

16. **Act of consecration to the Sacred Heart of Jesus and the Immaculate Heart of Mary.**

"Lord Jesus, Chief Shepherd of the flock, I consecrate myself to Your most Sacred Heart. From Your pierced Heart the Church was born, the Church You have called me, as a member of Shepherds of Christ Associates, to serve in a most special way. You reveal Your Heart as a symbol of Your love in all its aspects, including Your most special love for me, whom You have chosen as Your companion in this most important work. Help me to always love You in return. Help me to give myself entirely to You. Help me always to pour out my life in love of God and neighbor! Heart of Jesus, I place my trust in You!

"Dear Blessed Virgin Mary, I consecrate myself to your maternal and Immaculate Heart, this Heart which is symbol of your life of love. You are the Mother of my Savior. You are also my Mother. You love me with a most special love as a member of Shepherds of Christ Associates, a movement created by your Son as a powerful instrument for the renewal of the Church and the world. In a return of love, I give myself entirely to your motherly love and protection. You followed Jesus perfectly. You are His first and perfect disciple. Teach me to imitate you in the putting on of Christ. Be my motherly intercessor so that, through your Immaculate Heart, I may be guided to an ever closer union with the pierced Heart of Jesus, Chief Shepherd of the flock."

17. **Daily Prayers.** All members should say the Holy Spirit prayer daily and make the act of consecration daily. They should also pray the rosary each day. They are encouraged to use the other above prayers as time allows.

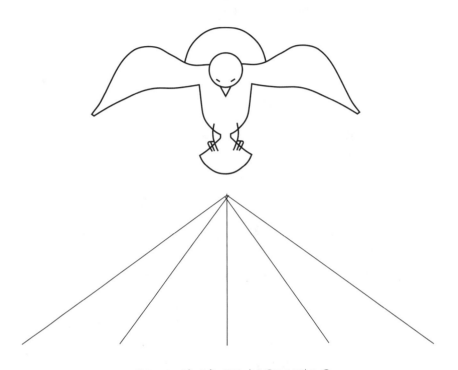

HOLY SPIRIT NOVENA

**The Holy Spirit Novnea prayers are
also available in
Spanish, French, and Portuguese.**

Shepherds of Christ Publications
China, Indiana

This book is published by Shepherds of Christ Publications, a subsidiary of Shepherds of Christ Ministries, a tax exempt religious public charitable association organized to foster devotion to the Two Hearts, the Sacred Heart of Jesus and the Immaculate Heart of Mary.

For additional copies, contact us:
Shepherds of Christ Ministries
P.O. Box 627
Madison (China), Indiana 47250 USA

(toll free number) 1-888-211-3041
(phone) 1-812-273-8405
(fax) 1-812-273-3182
http://www.SofC.org

Nihil Obstat:
Rev. Daniel J. Mahan, S.T.L.
Censor Librorum
Archdiocese of Indianapolis
Imprimatur:
Archbishop Daniel M. Buechlein, O.S.B.
Archbishop of Indianapolis
Archdiocese of Indianapolis

First Printing: March, 1999
Second Printing: April, 2000

DAILY NOVENA PRAYERS

Opening Prayer

In the name of the Father and of the Son and of the Holy Spirit. Amen.

Dear Father, we come to You in the name of Jesus, in union with Him in the Holy Sacrifice of the Mass, in the Holy Spirit. We come to You united to the Child Jesus of Good Health and the Infant of Prague. We come to You in the perfect, sinless heart of Our Mother Mary, asking her powerful intercession, uniting ourselves to her holy tears. We come to You united to all the angels and saints, and the souls in purgatory.

Prayer for Holy Spirit

We pray for an outpouring of the Holy Spirit on us, to be baptized by the Holy Spirit, that He will descend mightily on us as He did on the Apostles at Pentecost. That the Holy Spirit will transform us from fear to fearlessness and that He will give us courage to do all the Father is asking of us to help bring about the Reign of the Sacred Heart and the triumph of Mary's Immaculate Heart. We pray for the Holy Spirit to descend mightily on the Jesuits and the Poor Clares on the Shepherds of Christ leaders and members and on the whole Body of Christ and the world.

Protection by the Blood of Jesus

We pray that the Blood of Jesus will be spread on us, everyone in our families, and the Shepherds of Christ Movement, that we will be able to move steadfastly ahead and be protected from the evil one.

Healing

We pray for healing in body, mind, and soul and generational healing in ourselves, in all members in our families, and in all members of the Shepherds of Christ Movement, the Jesuit Community, the Poor Clares, the Body of Christ, and the world.

Prayer for Strength and Light

We adore You, oh Holy Spirit. Give us strength, give us light, console us. We give ourselves entirely to You. Oh Spirit of light and grace, we want to only do the will of the Father. Enlighten us that we may live always in the Father's will.

Eternal Spirit fill us with Your Divine Wisdom that we may comprehend more fully insight into Your Divine Mysteries.

Give us lights, Oh Holy Spirit that we may know God. Work within the heart, the spiritual womb of the Virgin Mary, to form us more and more into the image of Jesus.

Prayer to Be One with God, Father, Son and Holy Spirit

We long for You, Oh Spirit of Light, we long to know God, we want to be one with Him, our Divine God. We want to be one with the Father, know Him as a Person most intimately. We want to know the beloved One, the Sacred Heart of Jesus, and live and dwell in Him at all times, every moment of our lives. We want to be one with You, Oh Spirit of Light, that You move in us in our every breath.

Prayer to Be One in Jesus

Let us experience life in the Sacred Heart of Jesus, so we can say as Saint Paul, "I have been crucified with Christ and yet I am alive; yet it is no longer I, but Christ living in me...." Let us live, united to the Mass, all through the day being one in Him. Let us be able to love and know in this elevated state of oneness with our God. We long for Thee, oh beauteous God, we love You, we love You, we love You. We praise You, worship You, honor You, adore You, and thank You, our beloved God, Father, Son, and Holy Spirit.

Prayer to Dwell in the Hearts of Jesus and Mary

We seek to be one in God, to live and dwell in the Hearts of Jesus and Mary, our little heaven on earth, to experience life in the all perfect, pure, sinless heart of our Mother. We want the Holy Spirit to move in us and to be united to Jesus as the Bridegroom of our souls and be a most perfect sacrifice offered to the Father at every moment as we unite in the Holy Sacrifice of the Mass around the world to help in the salvation of souls.

Prayer for the Holy Spirit and His Gifts

Come Holy Spirit, come, come into our hearts, inflame all people with the fire of Your love.

Leader: Send forth Your Spirit and all will be reborn.

All: And You will renew the face of the earth.

We pray for the seven gifts of the Holy Spirit, we ask for perfection in our souls to make us holy, holy souls likened to God.

Dear Holy Spirit, we give ourselves to You soul and body. We ask You to give us the Spirit of Wisdom, Understanding, Counsel, Fortitude, Knowledge, Piety, and Fear of the Lord.

Prayer for the Word Alive in Our Hearts

We know, dear Holy Spirit, the Word in His human nature was brought forth within the womb of the woman. We pray that His word will be brought forth in our hearts as He lives and dwells in us. We want the incarnation to go on in our lives. Dear Holy Spirit, work in us.

Little Prayers to the Holy Spirit

Dear Holy Spirit, help us not to be ignorant or indifferent or weak, help us to be strong with the love of God.

Dear Holy Spirit, please pray for our needs for us.

Dear Holy Spirit, help us to respect God and to avoid sin. Help us to live in the Father's will.

Dear Holy Spirit, help us to keep Your commandments and to respect authority. Help us to love all things as You will us to love them. Help us to want to pray and always serve God with the greatest love. Help us to know the truth. Help us to have the gift of faith, hope, and love. Help us to know what is right and what is wrong.

A Prayer for Intimacy with the Lamb, the Bridegroom of the Soul

Oh Lamb of God, Who take away the sins of the world, come and act on my soul most intimately. I surrender myself, as I ask for the grace to let go, to just be as I exist in You and You act most intimately on my soul. You are the Initiator. I am the soul waiting Your favors as You act in me. I love You. I adore You. I worship You. Come and possess my soul with Your Divine Grace, as I experience You most intimately.

FIRST WEEK
MEDITATIONS NINE DAYS

1. **Romans 8:14-17**

All who are guided by the Spirit of God are sons of God; for what you received was not the spirit of slavery to bring you back into fear; you received the Spirit of adoption, enabling us to cry out, 'Abba, Father!' The Spirit himself joins with our spirit to bear witness that we are children of God. And if we are children, then we are heirs, heirs of God and joint-heirs with Christ, provided that we share his suffering, so as to share his glory.

2. **Romans 8:5-9**

Those who are living by their natural inclinations have their minds on the things human nature desires; those who live in the Spirit have their minds on spiritual things. And human nature has nothing to look forward to but death, while the Spirit looks forward to life and peace, because the outlook of disordered human nature is opposed to God, since it does not submit to God's Law, and indeed it cannot, and those who live by their natural inclinations can never be pleasing to God. You, however, live not by your natural inclinations, but by the Spirit, since the Spirit of God has made a home in you. Indeed, anyone who does not have the Spirit of Christ does not belong to him.

3. **1 John 4:12-16**

No one has ever seen God, but as long as we love one another God remains in us and his love comes to its perfection in us. This is the proof that we remain in him and he in us, that he has given us a share in his Spirit. We ourselves have seen and testify that the Father sent his Son as Saviour of the world. Anyone who acknowledges that Jesus is the Son of God, God remains in him and he in God. We have recognised for ourselves, and put our faith in, the love God has for us. God is love, and whoever remains in love remains in God and God in him.

4. 1 John 4:17-21
Love comes to its perfection in us when we can face the Day of Judgement fearlessly, because even in this world we have become as he is. In love there is no room for fear, but perfect love drives out fear, because fear implies punishment and no one who is afraid has come to perfection in love. Let us love, then, because he first loved us. Anyone who says 'I love God' and hates his brother, is a liar, since whoever does not love the brother whom he can see cannot love God whom he has not seen. Indeed this is the commandment we have received from him, that whoever loves God, must also love his brother.

5. 1 John 4:7-11
My dear friends, let us love one another, since love is from God and everyone who loves is a child of God and knows God. Whoever fails to love does not know God, because God is love. This is the revelation of God's love for us, that God sent his only Son into the world that we might have life through him. Love consists in this: it is not we who loved God, but God loved us and sent his Son to expiate our sins. My dear friends, if God loved us so much, we too should love one another.

6. Acts of the Apostles 1:1-5
In my earlier work, Theophilus, I dealt with everything Jesus had done and taught from the beginning until the day he gave his instructions to the apostles he had chosen through the Holy Spirit, and was taken up to heaven. He had shown himself alive to them after his Passion by many demonstrations: for forty days he had continued to appear to them and tell them about the kingdom of God. While at table with them, he had told them not to leave Jerusalem,

but to wait there for what the Father had promised. 'It is', he had said, 'what you have heard me speak about: John baptised with water but, not many days from now, you are going to be baptised with the Holy Spirit.'

7. Acts of the Apostles 1:6-9
Now having met together, they asked him, 'Lord, has the time come for you to restore the kingdom to Israel?' He replied, 'It is not for you to know times or dates that the Father has decided by his own authority, but you will receive the power of the Holy Spirit which will come on you, and then you will be my witnesses not only in Jerusalem but throughout Judaea and Samaria, and indeed to earth's remotest end.'

As he said this he was lifted up while they looked on, and a cloud took him from their sight.

8. Acts of the Apostles 1:12-14
So from the Mount of Olives, as it is called, they went back to Jerusalem, a short distance away, no more than a Sabbath walk; and when they reached the city they went to the upper room where they were staying; there were Peter and John, James and Andrew, Philip and Thomas, Bartholomew and Matthew, James son of Alphaeus and Simon the Zealot, and Jude son of James. With one heart all these joined constantly in prayer, together with some women, including Mary the mother of Jesus, and with his brothers.

9. Acts of the Apostles 2:1-4
When Pentecost day came round, they had all met together, when suddenly there came from heaven a sound as of a violent wind which filled the entire house in which they were sitting; and there appeared to them tongues as of fire; these separated and came to rest on the head of each of them. They were all filled with the Holy Spirit and began to speak different languages as the Spirit gave them power to express themselves.

SECOND WEEK
MEDITATIONS NINE DAYS

1. John 14:21-31

Whoever holds to my commandments and keeps them is the one who loves me; and whoever loves me will be loved by my Father, and I shall love him and reveal myself to him.'

Judas—not Judas Iscariot—said to him, 'Lord, what has happened, that you intend to show yourself to us and not to the world?' Jesus replied:

'Anyone who loves me will keep my word, and my Father will love him, and we shall come to him and make a home in him. Anyone who does not love me does not keep my words. And the word that you hear is not my own: it is the word of the Father who sent me. I have said these things to you while still with you; but the Paraclete, the Holy Spirit, whom the Father will send in my name, will teach you everything and remind you of all I have said to you. Peace I bequeath to you, my own peace I give you, a peace which the world cannot give, this is my gift to you. Do not let your hearts be troubled or afraid. You heard me say: I am going away and shall return. If you loved me you would be glad that I am going to the Father, for the Father is greater than I. I have told you this now, before it happens, so that when it does happen you may believe.

'I shall not talk to you much longer, because the prince of this world is on his way. He has no power over me, but the world must recognise that I love the Father and that I act just as the Father commanded. Come now, let us go.

2. John 17:11-26

I am no longer in the world, but they are in the world, and I am coming to you. Holy Father, keep those you have given me true to your name, so that they may be one like us. While I was with them, I kept those you had given me true to your name. I have watched over them and not one is lost except one who was destined to be lost, and this was to fulfil the scriptures. But now I am coming to you and I say these things in the world to share my joy with them to the full. I passed your word on to them, and the world hated them, because they belong to the world no more than I belong to the world. I am not asking you to remove them from the world, but to protect them from the Evil One. They do not belong to the world any more than I belong to the world. Consecrate them in the truth; your word is truth. As you sent me into the world, I have sent them into the world, and for their sake I consecrate myself so that they too may be consecrated in truth. I pray not only for these but also for those who through their teaching will come to believe in me. May they all be one, just as, Father, you are in me and I am in you, so that they also may be in us, so that the world may believe it was you who sent me. I have given them the glory you gave to me, that they may be one as we are one. With me in them and you in me, may they be so perfected in unity that the world will recognise that it was you who sent me and that you have loved them as you have loved me.

Father, I want those you have given me to be with me where I am, so that they may always see my glory which you have given me because you loved me before the foundation of the world. Father, Upright One, the world has not known you, but I have known you, and these have known that you have sent me. I have made your name known to them and will continue to make it known, so that the love with which you loved me may be in them, and so that I may be in them.

3. 1 Corinthians 15:20-28

In fact, however, Christ has been raised from the dead, as the first-fruits of all who have fallen asleep. As it was by one man that death came, so through one man has come the resurrection of the dead. Just as all die in Adam, so in Christ all will be brought to life; but all of them in their proper order: Christ the first-fruits, and next, at his coming, those who belong to him. After that will come the end, when he will hand over the kingdom to God the Father, having abolished every principality, every ruling force and power. For he is to be king until he has made his enemies his footstool, and the last of the enemies to be done away with is death, for he has put all things under his feet. But when it is said everything is subjected, this obviously cannot include the One who subjected everything to him. When everything has been subjected to him, then the Son himself will be subjected to the One who has subjected everything to him, so that God may be all in all.

4. Revelation 3:1-3,12,16-19

'Write to the angel of the church in Sardis and say, "Here is the message of the one who holds the seven spirits of God and the seven stars: I know about your behaviour: how you are reputed to be alive and yet are dead. Wake up; put some resolve into what little vigour you have left: it is dying fast. So far I have failed to notice anything in your behaviour that my God could possibly call perfect; remember how you first heard the message. Hold on to that. Repent! If you do not wake up, I shall come to you like a thief, and you will have no idea at what hour I shall come upon you.

Anyone who proves victorious I will make into a pillar in the sanctuary of my God, and it will stay there for ever; I will inscribe on it the name of my God and the name of the city of my God, the new Jerusalem which is coming down from my God in heaven, and my own new name as well.

'...but since you are neither hot nor cold, but only lukewarm, I will spit you out of my mouth. You say to yourself: I am rich, I have made a fortune and have everything I want, never realising that you are wretchedly and pitiably poor, and blind and naked too. I warn you, buy from me the gold that has been tested in the fire to make you truly rich, and white robes to clothe you and hide your shameful nakedness, and ointment to put on your eyes to enable you to see. I reprove and train those whom I love: so repent in real earnest.'

5. **Revelation 5:9-14**

They sang a new hymn: You are worthy to take the scroll and to break its seals, because you were sacrificed, and with your blood you bought people for God of every race, language, people and nation and made them a line of kings and priests for God, to rule the world.

In my vision, I heard the sound of an immense number of angels gathered round the throne and the living creatures and the elders; there were ten thousand times ten thousand of them and thousands upon thousands, loudly chanting:

Worthy is the Lamb that was sacrificed to receive power, riches, wisdom, strength, honour, glory and blessing. Then I heard all the living things in creation—everything that lives in heaven, and on earth, and under the earth, and in the sea, crying:

To the One seated on the throne and to the Lamb, be all praise, honour, glory and power, for ever and ever.

And the four living creatures said, 'Amen'; and the elders prostrated themselves to worship.

6. **Revelation 7:14-17**

I answered him, 'You can tell me, sir.' Then he said, 'These are the people who have been through the great trial; they have washed their robes white again in the blood of the Lamb. That is why they are standing in front of God's throne and serving him day and night in his sanctuary; and the One who sits on the throne will spread his tent over them. They will never hunger or thirst again; sun and scorching wind will never plague them, because the Lamb who is at the heart of the throne will be their shepherd and will guide them to springs of living water; and God will wipe away all tears from their eyes.'

7. Revelation 12:1-8

Now a great sign appeared in heaven: a woman, robed with the sun, standing on the moon, and on her head a crown of twelve stars. She was pregnant, and in labour, crying aloud in the pangs of childbirth. Then a second sign appeared in the sky: there was a huge red dragon with seven heads and ten horns, and each of the seven heads crowned with a coronet. Its tail swept a third of the stars from the sky and hurled them to the ground, and the dragon stopped in front of the woman as she was at the point of giving birth, so that it could eat the child as soon as it was born. The woman was delivered of a boy, the son who was to rule all the nations with an iron sceptre, and the child was taken straight up to God and to his throne, while the woman escaped into the desert, where God had prepared a place for her to be looked after for twelve hundred and sixty days.

And now war broke out in heaven, when Michael with his angels attacked the dragon. The dragon fought back with his angels, but they were defeated and driven out of heaven.

8. Revelation 14:1-7

Next in my vision I saw Mount Zion, and standing on it the Lamb who had with him a hundred and forty-four thousand people, all with his name and his Father's name written on their foreheads. I heard a sound coming out of heaven like the sound of the ocean or the roar of thunder; it was like the sound of harpists playing their harps. There before the throne they were singing a new hymn in the presence of the four living creatures and the elders, a hymn that could be learnt only by the hundred and forty-four thousand who had been redeemed from the world. These are the sons who have kept their virginity and not been defiled with women; they follow the Lamb wherever he goes; they, out of all people, have been redeemed to be the first-fruits for God and for the Lamb. No lie was found in their mouths and no fault can be found in them.

Then I saw another angel, flying high overhead, sent to announce the gospel of eternity to all who live on the earth, every nation, race, language and tribe. He was calling, 'Fear God and glorify him, because the time has come for him to sit in judgement; worship the maker of heaven and earth and sea and the springs of water.'

Revelation 19: 7-8
let us be glad and joyful and give glory to God, because this is the time for the marriage of the Lamb. His bride is ready, and she has been able to dress herself in dazzling white linen, because her linen is made of the good deeds of the saints.'

9. Revelation 21:1-10
Then I saw a new heaven and a new earth; the first heaven and the first earth had disappeared now, and there was no longer any sea. I saw the holy city, the new Jerusalem, coming down out of heaven from God, prepared as a bride dressed for her husband. Then I heard a loud voice call from the throne, 'Look, here God lives among human beings. He will make his home among them; they will be his people, and he will be their God, God-with-them. He will wipe away all tears from their eyes; there will be no more death, and no more mourning or sadness or

pain. The world of the past has gone.'
Then the One sitting on the throne spoke. 'Look, I am making the whole of creation new. Write this, "What I am saying is trustworthy and will come true."' Then he said to me, 'It has already happened. I am the Alpha and the Omega, the Beginning and the End. I will give water from the well of life free to anybody who is thirsty; anyone who proves victorious will inherit these things; and I will be his God and he will be my son. But the legacy for cowards, for those who break their word, or worship obscenities, for murderers and the sexually immoral, and for sorcerers, worshippers of false gods or any other sort of liars, is the second death in the burning lake of sulphur.'

One of the seven angels that had the seven bowls full of the seven final plagues came to speak to me and said, 'Come here and I will show you the bride that the Lamb has married.' In the spirit, he carried me to the top of a very high mountain, and showed me Jerusalem, the holy city, coming down out of heaven from God.

Revelation 22:20
The one who attests these things says: I am indeed coming soon.
Amen; come, Lord Jesus.

 Scriptural quotations are taken from
The New Jerusalem Bible, Doubleday & Co.
Imprimatur granted by Cardinal Hume.

Prayer for Union with Jesus

Come to me, Lord, and possess my soul. Come into my heart and permeate my soul. Help me to sit in silence with You and let You work in my heart. I am Yours to possess. I am Yours to use. I want to be selfless and only exist in You. Help me to spoon out all that is me and be an empty vessel ready to be filled by You. Help me to die to myself and live only for You. Use me as You will. Let me never draw my attention back to myself. I only want to operate as You do, dwelling within me.

I am Yours, Lord. I want to have my life in You. I want to do the will of the Father. Give me the strength to put aside the world and let You operate my very being. Help me to act as You desire. Strengthen me against the distractions of the devil to take me from Your work.

When I worry, I have taken my focus off of You and placed it on myself. Help me not to give in to the promptings of others to change what in my heart You are making very clear to me. I worship You, I adore You and I love You. Come and dwell in me now.

150 Year Celebration of St Boniface as a Parish and Father Joe's 50th Celebration of Ordination

IN REMEMBRANCE
OF MY
FIFTIETH ANNIVERSARY
OF PRIESTLY ORDINATION

REV. JOSEPH A. ROBINSON
1964   MAY   2014

Let us Pray for one another

Baptism

Eucharist

Confirmation

Confirmation

Marriage

Rita Robinson Ring and Fr. Joseph Robinson

Other great books published by Shepherds of Christ Publications

(To order call or write us at address in front of book)

Shepherds of Christ Prayer Manual The Shepherds of Christ has prayer chapters all over the world praying for the priests, the Church and the world. These prayers that Father Carter compiled in the summer of 1994 began this worldwide network of prayer. Currently the prayers are in eight languages with the Church's *Imprimatur.* We have prayed daily for the priests, the Church, and the world since 1994. Associates are called to join prayer Chapters and help us circulate the newsletter centered on spreading devotion to the Sacred Heart and Immaculate Heart and helping to renew the Church through greater holiness. Please form a Prayer Chapter & order a Prayer Manual. Item P1 - $0.50

Spirituality Handbook Fr. Edward Carter, S.J. did 3 synopsis of the spiritual life. *The Spirituality Handbook, the Priestly Newsletter 2000 Issue 3* and the *Tell My People* book. The way of spiritual life proposed to the members of Shepherds of Christ Associates is centered in consecration to the Hearts of Jesus and Mary. All aspects of the spiritual life discussed below should be viewed as means to help members develop their lives in consecration to Christ, the Sacred Heart, and to Mary, the Immaculate Heart. Item P2 - $3

Fr. Edward J. Carter S.J.

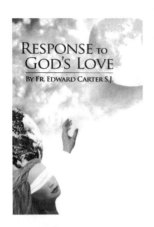

Response to God's Love by Fr. Edward J. Carter, S.J. In this book Fr. Carter speaks of God as the ultimate mystery. We can meditate on the interior life of the Trinity. Fr. Carter tells us about our uniqueness in the Father's Plan for us, how the individual Christian, the Church and the world are in the state of becoming. *Imprimatur*. Item BN4 -$10

Shepherds of Christ - Selected Writings on Spirituality for all People as Published in Shepherds of Christ Newsletter for Priests. Contains 12 issues of the newsletter from July/August 1994 to May/June 1996. Item BN1 - $15

Shepherds of Christ - Volume 2 by Fr. Edward J. Carter, S.J. Contains issues 13-29 of the Priestly newsletter (September / October 1996 - Issue 5, 1999) Item BN2 - $15

Fr. Edward J. Carter S.J.

Shepherds of Christ - Volume 3 by Fr. Edward J. Carter, S.J. Contains Priestly Newsletter Issues 1 through 4 of 2000 including Fr. Carter's tremendous *Overview of the Spiritual Life*
Item BN3 - $10

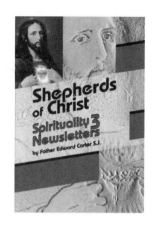

Rita Ring

Mass Book, by Rita Ring. Many of the entries in the Priestly Newsletter Volume II from a spiritual journal came from this book. These entries are to help people to be more deeply united to God in the Mass. This book is available in English and Spanish with the Church's *Imprimatur*.
Item B8 - $12

Parents and Children's Rosary Book, by Rita Ring. Short Meditations for both parents and children to be used when praying the rosary. These medi-tations will help all to know the lives of Jesus and Mary alive in their Hearts. Available in both English and Spanish with the Church's *Imprimatur*.
Item B7 - $10

Fr. Joe Robinson
(Rita Ring's Brother)

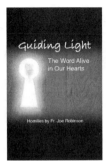

Guiding Light - The Word Alive in Our Hearts. - Cycle A (partial) — Homilies by the Reverend Joe Robinson given at St. Boniface Church in Cincinnati, Ohio. It is a tremendous honor Fr. Joe has allowed us to share these great gifts with you – for greater holiness and knowing more and more about God. Item C1 - $5

Guiding Light - Focusing on the Word - Cycle B — At times we may feel that our path to Christ is a bit "out of focus". Like the disciples in the Book of Mark, this ordinary life clouds our vision of Christ's Divinity. We may doubt the practicality or possibility of applying His teachings and example to our modern life. Cycle B's homilies are a "guiding light" to help us realize Jesus' Messianic greatness and His promise of better things to come. Item C2 - $15

Feed My Soul - Cycle C — In a world rapidly advancing and encouraging personal gain, we are faced with modern problems. There is a challenge to find time in our busy schedules for Sunday Mass or a family meal. We are able to research, shop, bank and even work without hearing one human voice. It is no wonder that we may often feel disconnected and famished at our week's end. In Fr. Joe's third book of homilies from Cycle C, we are reminded of the charity that Christ intended us to show each other. .... We are rewarded with the Father's kingdom and love when we are not worthy. We are not left alone or hungry. C3 - $15

Steadfast to the Son - Cycle A — The sunflower is a great example of how we should be steadfastly guided by light. What a powerful thought that this exceptional plant is not stuck in one pose day in and day out, yet adaptable and magnetized to the sun. We feel the same about our Son. Our heads turns to face Christ as each day presents its challenges to find light. We join together like plants in a field and soak up the Son through the pulpit. We are a warm circle of strength using the wind of our breath to carry our priests' words, Christ's words, to new rich soil. Item C4 - $15

Guiding Light - Reflect on the Word - Cycle B —
The Word leaves an impression on our souls. In my
thoughts and reflections are born a more tangible
understanding of these eternal concepts presented in
the Gospels and the readings. Anyone can read a
sentence, but not anyone can absorb it's true
meaning. Truth, in this day and age, is almost a
matter of opinion or individual entitlement. We
believe that Christ's truth is our Roman Catholic
Church. We, as priests, champion it's teachings; we
are ambassadors for the Pope and Christ to those
faces looking at us. We are the light by which our
congregation reads to reflect upon real truth and we
do it hand in hand. Item C5 - $15

Guiding Light - Centered In Christ, Cycle C — In
the gospel of St. Luke, Christ turns toward
Jerusalem, making   the choice of love through
sacrifice. In the silence of our own hearts, we find a
worthy call to action. What personal path will you
chose as you center in Jesus Christ? Fr. Joseph
Robinson has dedicated his life to serving Christ
and the Church from the Cincinnati Archdiocese
in Ohio for over 40 years. He inspires his
parishioners with the homilies found in these pages.
... May they be a guiding light for you as they have
been for so many others. Item C6 -$10

Guiding Light - Inspired To Be Genuine, Cycle A

We look over the pulpit, like a father over Sunday
breakfast and we want to connect. We want our
parishioners to know the fulfillment, wisdom and
desire that inspired our vows. We want them to find
Christ and each other in Christ. Like a father, we want
their attention, love and respect.

Privately, their minds may be else-where: in the
next meeting, compiling a grocery list, worrying about
a child, or angry with their spouse. We all leave a
proverbial tornado of obligatory noise at the church doors to enjoy a
single hour of unhurried glory. ... Father Joe Robinson inspires this
appreciation into focus with humor, interesting facts and fresh
perspectives. His homilies are easily followed, yet "meaty". May we all
succeed to enliven a tangible God in the heart's forefront of those who
hear us. Item C7 - $10

Featured Selections

Response in Christ by Fr. Carter

The book, **Response in Christ,** comes at a very opportune time. In a thoughtful blend of the traditional and the modern, Fr. Carter gives to the modern Christian a message that will sustain him.

The most promising aspect of the book is Fr. Carter's gift about the Spiritual life. The Christian life essentially consists in God's loving self-communication to us with our response to Him in love. God gives us a sharing in His life in baptism. This life is nourished by the Eucharist. Father Carter offers reflections on how to deepen one's relationship with God: Father, Son and Holy Spirit. Item BN5 -$10

By God Through Me by Fr. Joe Robinson

It can be challenging to remain alive to the magnitude of the role that I perform as a priest, a servant of God, a shepherd to the world, a sacramental sign of Christ... I wake up, eat, brush my teeth, get dressed and then transform bread into Flesh and wine into Blood.

Each Sunday, I look into all those faces. One is given new life by God through me in Baptism. Another is forgiven by God through me in Reconciliation. They are all loved by God through me. A troubled mother-to-be guided by God through me. My words can impact life or death decisions! This reality can sometimes seem surreal, but the glory remains, whether I am in the moment or not. May we all be blessed with mindfulness and a thankful nature. May these pages, in full or in part, provide a springboard to captivate your flock! May God bless you as a guiding light to all. -$10

We pray for you from our Church in China,
24 hours a day before the exposed Eucharist.
We pray eight-day retreats for you every month.

Shepherds of Christ Ministries

(You may copy this page to order.)

<u>Send Order To:</u>
Shepherds of Christ Ministries
P.O. Box 627
Madison (China), Indiana 47250 USA

Order Form

	Qty	Total $
P1. Prayer Manuals ($0.50)	___	_____
P2. Spirituality Handbook ($3)	___	_____
BN1. Shepherds of Christ - Volume 1 ($15)	___	_____
BN2. Shepherds of Christ - Volume 2 ($15)	___	_____
BN3. Shepherds of Christ - Volume 3 ($10)	___	_____
BN4. Response to God's Love ($10)	___	_____
BN5. Response in Christ ($10)	___	_____
B7. Parents and Children's Rosary Book($10)	___	_____
B8. Mass Book ($12)	___	_____
C1. The Word Alive in Our Hearts ($5)	___	_____
C2. Focusing on the Word - Cycle B ($15)	___	_____
C3. Feed My Soul - Cycle C ($15)	___	_____
C4. Steadfast to the Son - Cycle A ($15)	___	_____
C5. Reflect on the Word - Cycle B ($15)	___	_____
C6. Centered in Christ - Cycle C ($10)	___	_____
C7. Inspired To Be Genuine - Cycle A ($10)	___	_____
C8. By God Through Me - Cycle B ($10)	___	_____
C9. Trust and Transform - Cycle C ($10)	___	_____
Totals:	___	_____

Name: _____

Address: _____

City: _____ State: _____ Zip: _____

For More Information Call Toll free USA: 1-888-211-3041